STUDY GUIDES
English
Year 6

LES RAY AND GILL BUDGELL

Contents

RISING STARS

Content grid

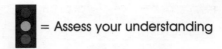 = Assess your understanding

Links to Primary Framework for Literacy Year 6

	Unit title	Focus text	Strand	Strand objective	Chat challenge
1	Spelling strategies – *i* before *e*	List of words featuring *ie* and *ei*	6 Word structure and spelling	Spell familiar words correctly and employ a range of strategies to spell difficult and unfamiliar words	Check understanding of terminology, purpose and links to spelling
2	Spelling strategies – derivation	Examples of word derivations in quiz format			Explore derivation and links to spelling
3	Mnemonics	Examples of common mnemonics			Check understanding of terminology, purpose and links to spelling
4	Editing, proofreading	'Poet Tree With Mist Aches' by Sauce unknown		Use a range of appropriate strategies to edit, proofread and correct spelling in their own work, on paper and on screen	Check understanding of terminology (homophones) and of process (edit and proofread)
5	▐ What have we learned?				
6	Point of view	Illustration of a car accident	7 Understanding and interpreting texts	Understand underlying themes, causes and points of view	Check on understanding of terminology and explore themes, causes and points of view together
7	Structures	*My East End*		Understand how writers use different structures to create coherence and impact	Check understanding of purpose and various techniques
8	Changing word meanings in different contexts	'American Folk Rhyme' adapted by William Cole		Explore how word meanings change when used in different contexts	Discuss what makes 'humorous misunderstanding' and explore purpose and audience
9	Devices to argue and persuade	Adapted from *Shooting the Elephant* by George Orwell		Recognise rhetorical devices used to argue, persuade, mislead and sway the reader	Discuss terminology, purpose, audience and key textual features
10	Cool reads	Reader review of *Soccer Mad* by Rob Childs	8 Engaging with and responding to texts	Read extensively and discuss personal reading with others, including in reading groups	Use as a basis for personalised discussion about 'cool' reads as well as what makes for a 'cool' review
11	Writers from different times	*Romeo and Juliet* in cartoon strip and original		Compare how writers from different times and places present experiences and use language	Use as a basis to compare how different treatments of text (time and place) affect accessibility
12	Writers from different places	*Little House in the Big Woods* by Laura Ingalls Wilder			Stress the need for textual evidence
13	▐ What have we learned?				

	Unit title	Focus text	Strand	Strand objective	Chat challenge
14	Narrative techniques – first person	*Animorphs 1, The Invasion* by K A Applegate	9 Creating and shaping texts	Using different narrative techniques to engage and entertain the reader	Check on understanding of terminology and explore 'speech' and story-telling together
15	Narrative techniques – third person	*Warrior Scarlet* by Rosemary Sutcliff			
16	Formal and informal writing – instructional	To grow crystals from a supersaturated solution		Select words and language drawing on their knowledge of literary features and formal and informal writing	Check on understanding of terminology, usage, purpose and effect
17	Formal and informal writing – biography	*Hannah Goslar Remembers* by Alison Leslie Gold			
18	Organising texts – diaries	*Zlata's Diary: A Child's Life in Sarajevo* by Zlata Filipovic		Use varied structures to shape and organise text coherently	Reconsider issues of narration, structure and formality in relation to usage, purpose and effect
19	Paragraphs	*Boo!* by Kevin Crossley-Holland	10 Text structure and organisation	Use paragraphs to achieve pace and emphasis	Revisit the usage, purpose and effect of paragraphs – even in extreme forms!
20	What have we learned?				
21	Argument – using sentences to persuade	Argument text: *Ban smoking! It kills!*	11 Sentence structure and punctuation	Express subtle distinctions of meaning, including hypothesis, speculation and supposition, by constructing sentences in varied ways	Check on understanding of terminology, usage, purpose and effect
22	Constructing sentences in varied ways 1	*Cider with Rosie* by Laurie Lee			
23	Constructing sentences in varied ways 2	*The Truth About Pets: Being Owned By a Cat*			
24	Colons or semicolons	*Walkabout* by James Vance Marshall		Use punctuation to clarify meaning in complex sentences	
25	Dashes or brackets	Adapted from *Pickwick Papers* by Charles Dickens			
26	Punctuation clarifying meaning	Examples of sentences punctuated differently			
27	Speech	*The Machine Gunners* by Robert Westall			
28	What have we learned?				

1 Spelling strategies – *i* before *e*

What strategies can you use to spell difficult words? Is learning a rule the only way?
Let's investigate.

> The rule: *i* before e except after c when the sound is 'ee'

Word bank

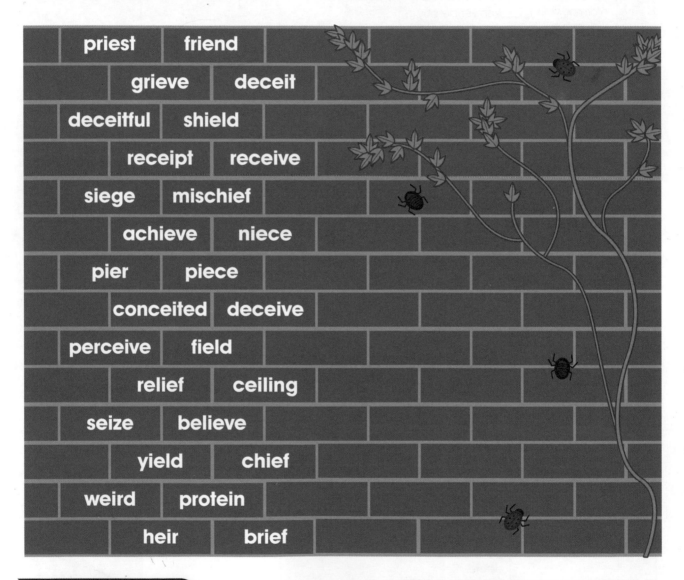

priest friend
grieve deceit
deceitful shield
receipt receive
siege mischief
achieve niece
pier piece
conceited deceive
perceive field
relief ceiling
seize believe
yield chief
weird protein
heir brief

Chat challenge

What do all of these words mean?
Do they follow the rule or not?
If they do not, can you explain why?
How can you remember the exceptions to the rule?
How many different sounds does *ie* make in these words?
What tips can you give to help spell these different-sounding words?

Comprehension

1) Which word means 'in love with yourself'?

2) Which word means 'the next in line to ...'?

3) Which words are derived from the same word roots?

4) Which words are exceptions to the rule?

5) Does a dictionary give you any helpful information to explain why?

6) In which words do *ie* or *ei* make a different sound to the others?

Objective focus

1) Rules are one strategy to help spelling – in this case with the sound of the word. One word in each pair is spelled incorrectly. Use the rule to find out which. Write it correctly.

    a. chief   freind   **c.** queit   priest

    b. theif   field   **d.** hieght   deceiver

2) Put *ie* or *ei* into the following words. Write them correctly.

    a. bel__ve   **c.** gr__f   **e.** conc__ve   **g.** rel__f

    b. y__ld   **d.** rec__ve   **f.** p__ce   **h.** rec__pt

3) Look closely at the letter that comes before *ie* or *ei* in the words in question 2. What is it in each case? Can you prove that the rule works?

4) How many exceptions can you find to the rule? E.g. **seize**.

Links to writing

1) One strategy to help with spelling is to look for patterns by breaking the word into syllables and pronouncing each part. Choose ten words from this unit. Break them into syllables and pronounce each one. Remember each syllable must have a vowel or a *y* sound.

2) Another strategy is to look for prefixes, suffixes or roots that you know. If you know how they work, it can make spelling easier. An etymological dictionary may help, e.g. *mis-* is a negative prefix and *re-* means **again**. Find examples in the list of words in this unit.

3) You can always use the *look, say, cover, write, check* strategy to learn the word.

Which do you find the most useful strategy and why?

2 Spelling strategies – derivation

Fred is stuck. He can't decide which are the right answers in this quiz about word derivation.

News gets its name from the first four letters of the four points of the compass – north, south, east and west. Information from all over the world.

*News from the Latin **noveles** meaning **new things**.*

Wellington named after the first Duke of Wellington. In military use in the 19th century, this was the high boot worn under the trousers.

Wellington boots to keep out the wet, invented when people had to clean out **wells**.

Alphabet named after the last two letters of the Latin alphabet. The word **alphabet** was first used by Roman children writing on their clay tablets.

*Alphabet named after the first two letters of the Latin alphabet: **alpha** and **beta** …*

Caravan a modern word for the vehicle which is towed behind a **car** or **van**.

*Caravan from the Persian **karwan**, meaning a group of desert travellers. The word later came to mean a covered cart for carrying passengers and goods.*

Far-fetched means **an unlikely story**. It comes from times when story-tellers roamed the land and they 'fetched' unlikely stories for people to hear.

*Far-fetched means an unlikely story. In the 16th century when the explorers used to return with strange things, they were known as **far-fetched goods**. They usually had a story to go with them which people seldom believed.*

Junk was at first a name for a Javanese sailing boat, **djong**, which often transported something of little value.

*Junk from the Latin word **juncus** meaning **reed**. Rope made from this was not very good and was known as **junk rope** as compared to better quality hemp rope.*

Gaffer The boss of an electrical team – he used to be in charge of the **gaff** (the place).

*Gaffer From an old English word for **grandfather**, a term of respect for someone with superior skills or someone who was your boss.*

The correct answers look like this.

Chat challenge

Are there any words that you do not know the meaning of? If so, look them up in a dictionary.

Does a dictionary always tell you the derivation of a word?

What kinds of words or symbols are used to tell you where the words originated?

Where would you look to find the derivation of a word?

How many different countries have provided us with the words here?

How many of the questions did you get right?

How can the derivation of a word help you with spelling?

Comprehension

1) Which words are derived from particular words in other languages?

2) Which words are derived from ideas of what happened in the past?

3) **Wellington** is derived from someone's name. Find out which words are derived in the following way:

    a. Scot who invented waterproof material

    b. Earl who invented snack out of bread

    c. US President Roosevelt who refused to kill large animals

4) Are there any of these words that we do not use today?

5) How do you think these words arrived in our country and so in our language from so far away?

 Objective focus

1) Find out how an etymological dictionary is different from one you have used.

2) Look at the prefixes of all these words. What do they tell you about the meaning of the words?

    a. unique   **b.** triangle   **c.** decimal   **d.** octet   **e.** biscuit

3) Find out more about the derivation of these groups of words below. From which countries did they originate?

    a. democracy, gymnasium, theatre, orchestra, atom

    b. movie, supermarket, teenagers, detergent, gangster

    c. hamburger, dachshund, lager, kindergarten, rucksack

 Links to writing

1) Investigate more words from different countries. You could link this with history work, e.g. **Which words did the Romans bring when they invaded?** (Latin and Greek) **What was the impact of the Viking invasion?** (Old Norse words, names of places) **What was the impact of the invasion of 1066?** (French words) Find examples of each of these.

2) Carry out a class survey to find out more about the derivation of your names, e.g. **Donna** is derived from the Italian for **lady**, **Neil** from the gaelic for **champion**. Surnames often have a derivation related to original occupation. Discuss how children from different cultures may have different ways of deriving names.

3 Mnemonics

People have invented strange ways to remember how to spell words! Which way do you find most helpful?

How to spell **arithmetic**?
A Rat **I**n **T**he **H**ouse **M**ay **E**at **T**he **I**ce **C**ream

How to spell **necessary**?
Never **E**at **C**ucumber **E**at **S**almon **S**andwiches **A**nd **R**emain **Y**oung

Mississippi
Say the word aloud in a special rhythm: (M ... I ... SS ... I ... SS ... I ... PP ... I)

Principal or **Principle**?
A princi**pal** at a school is your **pal**, and a princip**le** you believe is a ru**le**.

There or **Their**?
Their – meaning **belonging to them**
There – meaning **in that place**
This can be remembered by **HERE** and **THERE** –
in that place is the one ending in the word **here**.

Put it over there!

It's theirs!

Separate is **A RAT** of a word to spell.

Sep a rat e

Would you rather have one **S** or two?
Twice as much for dessert!
deSSert – two **s**; **desert** – one **s**.
When you eat **dessert**, you always want to
come back for the second **s**.

Rhythm **h**as **y**our **t**wo **h**ands **m**oving!

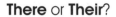

Chat challenge

What is a **mnemonic**?
From which language is it derived? You may have to use a dictionary.
What spelling problems do the mnemonics help to solve?
How is the mnemonic for **arithmetic** different from the one for **principal**?
How is the mnemonic for **Mississippi** different from the one for **dessert**?
Do you have any favourite mnemonics?

Comprehension

1) Look at the examples. Which mnemonics do you find the most helpful in spelling difficult words?

2) Which mnemonics make you break down the words and look more closely at how they are made up?

3) Which mnemonics concentrate on the letters in a word? Do any concentrate on the sounds of the words?

4) Which mnemonics do you find most helpful in remembering difficult ideas?

5) How do the drawings help you to remember the words?

Objective focus

1) Mnemonics are ways we invent to help us to remember something. One way is to find a word 'inside' a difficult word and make up a short story about it. Which words do you think these mnemonics help you to spell?

   a. It caused me ANGER. Now I'm very d _ _ _ _ _ _ s

   b. I like PIE. Give me a p _ _ _ e

   c. ATE all my beautiful creamy ch _ _ _ _ _ e

2) Find smaller words in these words and think of mnemonics. Each mnemonic can be individual. There is no right answer.

   a. wonderful   **b** height   **c.** vegetable   **d.** practice   **e.** juice

3) Some people use the letters of each word to make a sentence (an acrostic), e.g. **R**hythm **h**as **y**our **t**wo **h**ands **m**oving! Write acrostics for these words.

   a. Wednesday   **b.** February   **c.** miniature

Links to writing

1) Some people find looking at a picture created by the word a helpful mnemonic. Draw some pictures incorporating the following words, that may help younger children to spell them:

   a. island   **b.** snake   **c.** centipede   **d.** giant

2) Invent some short stories to help spell difficult words, e.g.:

   Every morning the *man goes* into his garden to pick *mangoes*.

3) Challenge each other to find as many smaller words as possible in larger words, e.g.:

   a. misshapen   **b.** loathsome   **c.** superintendent   **d.** rebellion

4 Editing, proofreading

Poet Tree With Mist Aches

I have a spelling chequer
It came with my pea sea
It plainly marquees four my revue
Miss steaks eye cannot sea.

Eye strike a quay and right a word
And weight four it two say
Weather eye am wrong oar write
It shows me strait away.

As soon as a mist ache is maid
It nose bee fore to late
And eye can putt the error rite
It's rarely, rarely great.

I've run this poem threw it
I'm shore your pleased too no
It's letter perfect in its weigh
My chequer tolled me sew.

Sauce unknown

Chat challenge

What is the poet using to write the poem?
What do you notice about the spelling in the poem?
What point is the poet trying to make?
How many of the spellings can you correct?
Why is the poem amusing?

Comprehension

1) A good way to edit and proofread is by using a highlighter. Photocopy the poem and mark any words which are incorrect.

2) Beside them write the correct version of the words if you know them.

3) Check your answers in your dictionary. You could look up any words that you do not know.

4) Take a verse. Put in some punctuation at the end of the lines. What would be the best to use? Compare your version with someone else and talk about the differences.

5) Write a correctly-spelled version of the poem using your computer. Take care with the spellchecker!

Objective focus

1) Homophones are words that sound the same but have different meanings and are spelled differently. Find ten examples in the poem.

2) Find other spellings for words that sound like:

    a. ate   **b.** sore   **c.** steel   **d.** tail   **e.** two

    f. there   **g.** bear   **h.** pour   **i.** rain   **j.** four

3) Use a dictionary to find the meanings of these words in the poem:

    a. marquees   **b.** quay   **c.** putt   **d.** rite   **e.** tolled

4) Find out more about homophones, homonyms and homographs. What is the difference between them? Use the Internet to research.

Links to writing

1) Write a list of helpful hints to someone who is just about to use a computer spellchecker, so that they avoid these problems.

2) Edit and present this in the most appropriate way. Print and display in the classroom.

3) You could present what you have found out about these strange words to the rest of the class. Make a PowerPoint presentation in a group.

4) Tell an amusing story based on a misunderstanding in spelling caused by a computer spellchecker.

Assess your
understanding

 OK

 OK but need
more practice

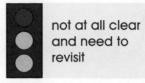 not at all clear
and need to
revisit

5 What have we learned?

We've learned about **word structure and spelling**.

1 How to use spelling strategies: *i* before e

● A basic rule can help to spell a tricky word – *i* before e except after c, but only when it (the *ie* or *ei*) rhymes with **ee**.

● There are always exceptions to rules – so beware.

● Other strategies include: breaking a word into syllables, making up a mnemonic and thinking about derivation.

● You can also just return to *look, say, cover, write, check*.

The exceptions
to this rule are:
**weird, weir, seize
and people's
names**

Check understanding!

Write out all the spelling rules you know with an example word for each.

2 How to use spelling strategies: using derivation

● **Derivation** means 'where something has come from'.

● An etymological dictionary will help you with derivation.

● Knowing where a root word comes from can help you with spelling a whole range of words, e.g. **specto** (I look).

Check understanding!

Prepare a test for a friend. Choose a word from each of the following and test your friend on the country or language, and the meaning. Ask them to think of an associated word too.

Language	Word	Meaning	Associated word
Latin			
Greek			
Hindi			
French			
(another of your choice)			

Assess your understanding

 OK

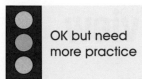 OK but need more practice

 not at all clear and need to revisit

3 How to use spelling tricks: mnemonics

- Some words are just tricky and it's worth making up your own rule. Remember '**b**ig **e**lephants **c**an **a**lways **u**nderstand **s**mall **e**lephants' from way back? That's because you made a mnemonic.

- Make them up just for you and then use them!

Check understanding!

 Write your own rule or mnemonic for these:

- practice/practise
- affect/effect
- dessert/desert
- of/off

- advice/advise
- there/their/they're
- too/two/to
- tomorrow

4 How to edit and proofread

- Reread your work to check the spellings and the grammar, but also check that:
  - the message of the writing is clear
  - the text type is clear with all the right features.
- When a word is a homophone be extra sure to check that you have the right version!

Check understanding!

 Check a piece of your own recent work and edit it using a highlighter pen and using the checks above.

The more you read the more words you will have in your head. The more words in your head, the more words you will be able to write.

When you hear or read something interesting – write it down and use it next time you are writing.

6 Point of view

Look at the picture of the accident. How would the different people tell the story?

Chat challenge

Who is involved directly in the accident?

How would they want to tell people about what happened?

For each of the points of view, if they had to write what they saw, who might their audience be?

What would be the purpose of their writing?

Would each account be similar or different? Why?

Comprehension

1) Describe what each person might see at the accident.

2) Is this influenced by where the person is positioned?

3) What other senses would be involved? What could each person say about these?

4) How much of each person's account can you believe as 'the whole truth'?

5) How will each point of view appeal to a different audience and therefore require a different style? Which versions will use the first person, the third person, the present tense, the past tense?

Objective focus

1) You are the police officer at the scene. Write what would be in your notebook describing the scene. Why is your statement written in this style? Is it factual?

2) You are the car driver (Mr Roberts). Tell the story of your day to your sister in conversation as she visits you in hospital. How is this different from the style of the police officer?

3) You are one of the firefighters. Tell your version of the incident. What style will the report be written in?

4) You are the newspaper reporter. Write the newspaper article that appears that evening in the local newspaper. Is it factual?

5) You are Mrs Roberts. Tell the story of how your husband's accident changed your day. Which facts would you choose to include?

Links to writing

1) Choose a newspaper article – it could be a sports review. Rewrite the news story from a completely different point of view.

Whose point of view will you choose?
What do they see, hear, feel?
How will it be different from the original?

2) Imagine that you are transformed into an animal for a day, e.g. a **cat**. Write about your adventures.

What will the world be like for you?
What is the world like to the animal – big, small, microscopic?
How does it deal with its surroundings?

7 Structures

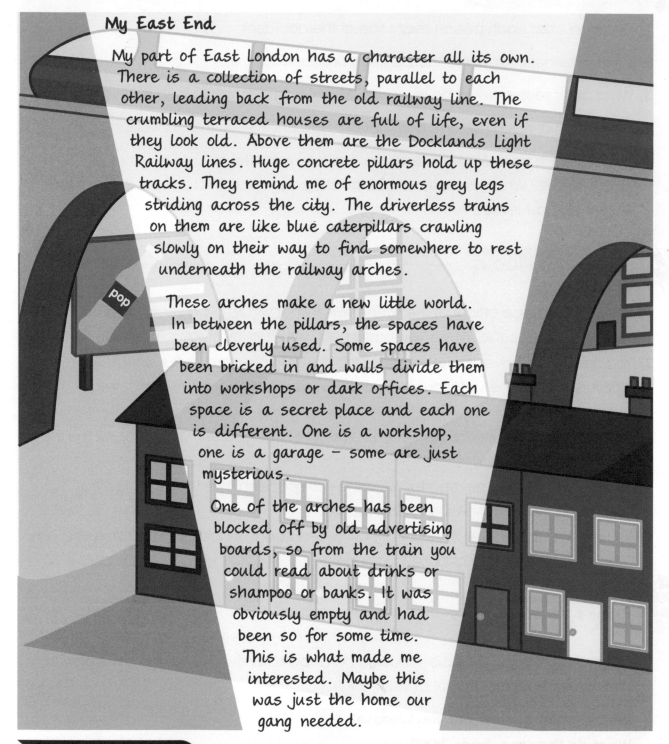

My East End

My part of East London has a character all its own. There is a collection of streets, parallel to each other, leading back from the old railway line. The crumbling terraced houses are full of life, even if they look old. Above them are the Docklands Light Railway lines. Huge concrete pillars hold up these tracks. They remind me of enormous grey legs striding across the city. The driverless trains on them are like blue caterpillars crawling slowly on their way to find somewhere to rest underneath the railway arches.

These arches make a new little world. In between the pillars, the spaces have been cleverly used. Some spaces have been bricked in and walls divide them into workshops or dark offices. Each space is a secret place and each one is different. One is a workshop, one is a garage – some are just mysterious.

One of the arches has been blocked off by old advertising boards, so from the train you could read about drinks or shampoo or banks. It was obviously empty and had been so for some time. This is what made me interested. Maybe this was just the home our gang needed.

Chat challenge

What is being described in each paragraph?
How is each paragraph very different in what it describes?
How does one paragraph link to another?
Why has the text been put into the shape that it has?
What do you think might be in the next paragraph if there is one?
Why do you think we talk about these paragraphs forming 'a structure'?

Comprehension

1) What does the first paragraph describe?

2) Find its topic sentence and the sentences which illustrate it.

3) What do the other two paragraphs describe?

4) Show how what is described keeps becoming smaller.

5) How do you know that this is a story and not an autobiography?

Objective focus

1) Continue with this story. Use the same paragraph structure – start large and get smaller.

Describe the arch from the outside and what the gang will do with it.

Go inside the arch and describe it.

Focus on a person in the room.

Use speech to say more about this person.

2) How and why is speech set out in paragraphs? What happens if it is not?

Links to writing

1) In this description, the writer starts looking from a wide angle and then focuses in on something smaller. Write a three-paragraph description of your school following the same plan.

In the first paragraph, describe the whole area and its features.

In the second paragraph, describe one part of this area.

In the third paragraph, describe one smaller thing in this part.

Use detail which will show you really know the area.

2) Edit your description to write the opening of a story about something really terrible that happens at your school. Like a film, have the long shot, medium shot and close-up happening within seconds for maximum effect.

3) You could find or take photographs of your area, and the parts of your area, to illustrate your writing.

8 Changing word meanings in different contexts

American Folk Rhyme

Where can a man buy a cap for his knee?

Or a key for the lock of his hair?

And can his eyes be called at school?

I would think – there are pupils there.

What jewels are found in the crown of his head,

And who walks on the bridge of his nose?

Can he use, in building the roof of his mouth,

The nails on the ends of his toes?

Can the crook of his elbow be sent to jail –

If it can, well, then what did it do?

And how does he sharpen his shoulder blades?

I'll be hanged if I know – do you?

Can he sit in the shade of the palm of his hand,

And beat time with the drum of his ear?

Can the calf of his leg eat the corn on his toe?

There's somethin' pretty strange around here!

Adapted by William Cole

Chat challenge

When you read this poem, what did you think was strange?
Explain why this poem is amusing.
Can you identify all the words that have two meanings depending in which context they are used?
Explain the different contexts that can make them mean different things.
Are there any words that you do not understand when they are used in another context?

Comprehension

1) What is the **bridge** of your nose? In what context is a **bridge** something else?

2) Where is the **crown** of your head? In what context is a **crown** something else?

3) What does an ear **drum** do?

4) Write sentences where each of these words means something different in another context.

Objective focus

1) Many words have two meanings, according to the context you use them in. Write sentences showing different meanings and contexts of these words:

   a. pine   **b.** rush   **c.** field   **d.** ball   **e.** match

2) Write sentences using these words in their original context and in a musical context:

   a. rock   **b.** album   **c.** band   **d.** pop

3) Write sentences using these words in their original context and in a cinema context:

   a. shot   **b.** still   **c.** film   **d.** location

4) In the following sentences, the context is set by the sentence but the wrong word has been chosen. Write each of the sentences correctly. Explain why they are amusing.

   a. I am the most populous person in the school.

   b. The River Nile irritates the land every year.

   c. I speak properly. I've taken electrocution lessons.

Links to writing

1) Plan a story about the confusion caused when words are used in the wrong context. You could use some examples from the poem.

   - How does the confusion arise?
   - Who is responsible?
   - What happens as a result?
   - How is the situation resolved?

   Use speech to make the most of the comedy. Show how people react.

2) Jokes are often the result of the same words being used in a wrong context. Survey the class to collect their jokes. How many are caused because of words used in an incorrect context?

9 Devices to argue and persuade

Adapted from *Shooting the Elephant*

Nearly all sports practised nowadays are competitive. You play to win, and the game has little meaning unless you do your utmost to win. On the village green, where you pick up sides and no feeling of local patriotism is involved, it is possible to play simply for the fun and exercise: but as soon as the question of prestige arises, as soon as you feel some larger unit will be disgraced if you lose, are not the most savage combative instincts aroused? Anyone who has played in a school football match knows this. At the international level, sport is frankly mimic warfare. But the significant thing is not the behaviour of the players but the attitude of the spectators, of the nations who work themselves into furies over these absurd contests …

As soon as strong feelings of rivalry are aroused, the notion of playing the game according to the rules always vanishes. People want to see one side on top and the other side humiliated, and they forget that victory gained through cheating or through the intervention of the crowd is meaningless. Even when the spectators don't intervene physically don't they try to influence the game by cheering their own side and 'rattling' opposing players with boos and insults? Serious sport has nothing to do with fair play. It is bound up with hatred, jealousy, boastfulness, disregard of all rules and sadistic pleasure in witnessing violence: in other words, it is war minus the shooting.

George Orwell

Chat challenge

What does the writer say is different between playing sport 'on the village green' and in a 'school football match'?

Do you think the writer approves of competitive sport? Why?

Do you agree with the writer's argument about sport?

Do you think there is a solution to the problem he talks about? If so what is it?

How do you know that the writer is trying to persuade you of his argument?

What kind of persuasive features can you identify in the passage?

Comprehension

1) Why do people play competitive sport?

2) What sort of attitudes does the author say it creates?

3) Are these attitudes good or bad? Can you think of any examples from when you have played or watched sport when things like this have happened? Give some examples and explain why you think things happened.

4) Who does the writer blame for this attitude: the players or the spectators?

5) What examples does the author give to prove that these people make things worse?

Objective focus

1) Find examples of the author using **you** in the passage. Is this direct appeal to the reader more persuasive than using **I**?

2) Writers of arguments also like to group people together to suggest that **everyone** believes the same as he or she does. Can you find examples of this in the passage?

3) Look at the way the writer starts some sentences in the argument: 'Even when … ' How do these words help to make the argument flow better?

4) Rhetorical questions are a special kind of question which, although they are 'asked', actually require no answer. We use them when we are trying to be persuasive. Find examples in the passage. How do you think they help in persuading you? How much do they involve you in the argument?

Links to writing

1) Write two paragraphs to argue that competitive sport is a good thing. Use the persuasive techniques that this unit shows.

Choose information to back up your arguments.

Create a personal relationship with the reader sometimes by using you, **in order to include them.**

Use statements or rhetorical questions to suggest that certain facts are absolutely correct.

Use words such as people **and** everyone **to suggest that we all believe the argument.**

Choose connectives carefully to link ideas logically: therefore … however … moreover … **and to make the argument develop.**

10 Cool reads

This review is by Jordan Sandford from Barnet, London. He wrote this review when he was 12 years old.

Soccer Mad

by Rob Childs

Corgi Learning, 1996, 120 pages, ISBN 0440863449

How easy was it to get stuck into this book?

This book is great and is easy to understand if you know about football.

Who are the main characters?

The book is about a young boy called Luke who isn't that good at football, but knows everything there is to know about the sport.

What's the storyline?

The story line is easy to follow. Luke has never played football for his school before but as the flu virus hits the school he finally gets his chance to play. But it doesn't go well, his captain Matthew is always putting Luke down but Luke just ignores him. Soon Luke's Sunday team Swifts draw Matthew's Sunday team the Panthers. The game is the most exciting part of the book, and believe it or not Luke's team win.

How's it written?

The book is written in chapters and with only 120 pages it won't take long to read.

Other books by the same author that Jordan Sandford knows about?

Soccer at Sandford, Sandford on tour, The big match, The big day, The big goal, The big kick, The big game, The big prize, The big chance, The big star, The big hit, The big freeze, The big break, All goalies are crazy, football daft, Football flukes.

The overall verdict is …

★★★★★ A cool-read

http://www.cool-reads.co.uk

Chat challenge

Why is Jordan writing about this book?

Who is his audience? What is he trying to achieve?

Where was the book published? Would this have any effect on the style?

What does he like about the book?

Did he see any drawbacks to it?

What do you notice about the way that the review has been written on the page?

Does this make it easier or more difficult to read? Explain why.

Comprehension

1) What does the cover of the book tell you?

2) Why do book reviews contain information such as the ISBN number?

3) What does the writer like most about the book?

4) What does the writer tell you about Luke?

5) Why does the writer say 'believe it or not Luke's team win'?

6) What's the biggest attraction to the writer about the way the book is written?

Objective focus

1) The book review comes from the Internet and has not been edited. Rewrite the paragraph 'What's the storyline?', paying more attention to full stops and commas.

2) Check your new version with a friend. Do they use the same punctuation?

3) In this paragraph, what is incorrect about 'Luke's team win'? Explain why.

4) Rewrite the paragraph listing other books by the same author. Pay attention to how titles should be punctuated and which words take capital letters. Check your new version with a friend. Do they use the same punctuation?

5) The review has a particular structure. List the headings. Which other headings would you add to make the review better, e.g.:

Things I didn't like about this book

Would I recommend it to a friend?

Links to writing

1) Using the structure identified above, write a book review.

Use the same amount of text and information as Jordan Sandford's review.

Use the same kind of language.

Set out your review using a computer: use fonts, spacing and other layout features to make the information clear.

2) Keep a reading journal for a few weeks.

Give important details about each book you read or look at for research.

Explain why you found it interesting or useful.

Which examples will you use to prove your points?

11 Writers from different times

Help! Fred has to read some of Shakespeare's
Romeo and Juliet in class!
He has found two versions.

Nurse: Madam, your mother craves a
word with you.

Romeo: What is her mother?

Nurse: Marry bachelor.
Her mother is the lady of the house,
And a good lady, and a wise and virtuous …

Romeo: Is she a Capulet?
O dear account! My life is my foe's debt.

(Exeunt all but Juliet and the Nurse)

Juliet: Come hither Nurse. What is yond
gentleman? … What's he that follows there,
that would not dance?

Nurse: I know not.

Juliet: Go ask his name. If he be married,
My grave is like to be my wedding bed.

Nurse: His name is Romeo, and a
Montague;
The only son of your great enemy.

Juliet: My only love sprung from my
only hate!

Chat challenge

Which version do you think is easier to understand? Why?
Which words in the original do you not understand?
In which period of history was Shakespeare writing?
How could you find out the meaning of the difficult words?
Do you know the rest of the story? How does it end?
Besides the language, what other things might make writers from the past difficult to
read and understand?
Look at another scene in Shakespeare's *Romeo and Juliet* to find the words he used.
How much of that scene do you understand? What can you use to help you?

Comprehension

1) In the cartoon version of the play, how can you tell who the characters are?

2) Who is the hero and who is the heroine of this story? How do you know?

3) In the cartoon, how do the pictures give you information besides the words the characters speak?

4) Does the cartoon use the same words as Shakespeare's original? What is left out?

5) In the playscript, how does Shakespeare tell you who is on stage?

6) How does Shakespeare tell the actors how to behave?

7) Can the playscript features be used in the cartoon version? Explain your answer.

Objective focus

1) Shakespeare wrote this in the 1590s. Language has changed since then. How would we say the following today?

    a. '… your mother craves a word with you.'

    b. 'Her mother is the lady of the house.'

    c. 'Come hither Nurse.'

    d. 'What is yond gentleman?'

2) Other words that we use have changed their original meaning. Find out what these words used to mean in the past.

    a. nice   **b.** villain   **c.** awful   **d.** horrid   **e.** naughty

    You may need to use an etymological dictionary or the Internet.

Links to writing

1) Find out more about the story of *Romeo and Juliet*. Choose one episode from it and produce it as a one-page cartoon story for people of your own age.

When you draw it, what clothes will they be wearing?

Where is the story set? This will determine the background of your pictures.

What words will you give the characters to say?

Will you use the language of the time?

12 Writers from different places

From *Little House in the Big Woods*

Laura and Mary had never seen a town. They had never seen a store. They had never seen even two houses standing together. But they knew that in a town there were many houses, and a store full of candy and calico and other wonderful things – powder, and shot, and salt, and store sugar.

They knew that Pa would trade his furs to the storekeeper for beautiful things from town, and all day they were expecting the presents he would bring them. When the sun sank low above the treetops and no more drops fell from the tips of the icicles they began to watch eagerly for Pa.

The sun sank out of sight, the woods grew dark, and he did not come. Ma started supper and set the table, but he did not come. It was time to do the chores, and still he had not come.

Ma said that Laura might come with her while she milked the cow. Laura could carry the lantern.

So Laura put on her coat and Ma buttoned it up. And Laura put her hands into the red mittens that hung by a red yarn string around her neck, while Ma lighted the candle in the lantern.

Laura was proud to be helping Ma with the milking, and she carried the lantern very carefully. Its sides were of tin, with places cut in them for the candle-light to shine through.

When Laura walked behind Ma on the path to the barn, the little bits of candle-light from the lantern leaped all around her on the snow. The night was not yet quite dark. The woods were dark, but there was a grey light on the snowy path, and in the sky there were a few faint stars. The stars did not look as warm and bright as the little lights that came from the lantern.

Laura was surprised to see the dark shape of Sukey, the brown cow, standing at the barnyard gate. Ma was surprised, too.

It was too early in the spring for Sukey to be let out in the Big Woods to eat grass. She lived in the barn. But sometimes on warm days Pa left the door of her stall open so she could come into the barnyard. Now Ma and Laura saw her behind the bars, waiting for them.

Laura Ingalls Wilder

Chat challenge

How do you know that this is probably set in another place, very different from where you live?

What kinds of things do the children have or not have?

How are these different from your experience?

What tells you that the story is also probably set in the past?

Are there any words that tell you this might be written by someone from another country?

What do you find unusual about how the children behave?

Comprehension

1) The children had never seen two houses standing together. What could this tell you about the kind of place they lived?

2) What kind of things did the children know were in town?

3) What did the children's father do in the stores?

4) What detail in the passage tells you about the season?

5) What kind of chores did the girls do?

6) Why were Ma and Laura surprised to see Sukey at the gate?

 Objective focus

1) The story is set in the pioneering days of the United States, in the Midwest during the mid-19th century. Research detail to create a sense of another place. You can make your writing more effective by concentrating on:

   the words that are spoken

   the comments you use to say how they are spoken

   the detail of the scene around you

   the events and places that they talk about.

2) Imagine that the girls go to town. Write about their first visit to a town.

   What do they see – the buildings, the streets, the people, their behaviour?

   What did they feel about it?

   How will you make the place come alive for your reader?

 Links to writing

1) Plan another story set in the Midwest. You could use the same characters and include some kind of problem or crisis.

   Once you have decided on your plot, write your story so that your reader finds out about details of life in the Midwest through the action or descriptions in the story, e.g.:

   daily life

   food and clothes

   ways of talking (any special words used).

Remember not to write descriptions of these points. You are not writing an account of life in the Midwest. You must give the reader a strong impression of the place as you tell the story.

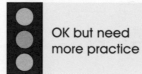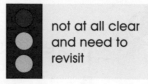

13 What have we learned?

We've learned how to **understand and interpret texts** and to **engage with and respond to text**.

1 How to take account of point of view

- Practising hot-seating or role-play helps to get inside a character's skin.
- It's important to see things from different points of view as they can often look very different.

Check understanding!

Think of the last time you were in trouble at school or at home. Tell or write it from your point of view and then (try really hard!) to tell it from your teacher's or parent's point of view.

2 How authors use structures to create impact

- You can start from the big picture and work down to the detail or vice versa.
- Use paragraphs to flag up the moving in or moving out.

Check understanding!

Try writing an opening to a story – beginning wide and narrowing and then vice versa.

3 How word meanings change in different contexts

- The meaning of words can change over time.
- Words used in the wrong context can be confusing or amusing.

Check understanding!

Find a joke book or an old-fashioned book. Find three examples of words that could have different meanings in a different context. What would the other context be?

Assess your understanding OK 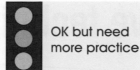 OK but need more practice 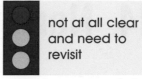 not at all clear and need to revisit

4 How to use devices to argue and persuade

- To persuade a reader, develop a logical argument from a particular viewpoint.
- Start with a question or a bold statement; use paragraphs in a logical order and that are linked; finish with a clear summary.

Check understanding!

Find a leaflet or an advertisement in a newspaper or magazine. Note all the devices that are used to argue and persuade you as a reader.

5 How to write book reviews

- Include facts about the book, e.g. title, author and a 'blurb' (description of the book).
- List main characters, the general theme and the storyline (but don't give the plot away).

Check understanding!

Write a review for a book you have recently read.

6 How to respond to writers from different times

- Language from the past can be made easier to read by simplifying the language, updating the language or by illustrating the story in a cartoon strip.

Check understanding!

Choose a nursery rhyme that you know, such as 'Humpty Dumpty' or 'London Bridge'. Research its origins. What did it mean in its original form? Who was it about?

7 How to respond to writers from different places

- A writer's experience of setting can influence their writing very strongly so that some writing has a very definite sense of place and is very personal.

Check understanding!

Write a paragraph about a place that is special to you. Give as many clues as possible so that your readers feel that they know something special about you.

14 Narrative techniques – first person

From *Animorphs 1, The invasion*

I did it Monday morning in my locker at school. I turned into a lizard.

I started to focus for the morphing. I remembered the way we had caught the lizard the night before last. We spotted it with a torch, and Cassie had put a bucket over it so it couldn't get away.

It had been fairly creepy, just touching it to acquire its DNA pattern. Now I was going to become it.

Things began to happen very fast. It was like falling. Like falling off a skyscraper and taking for ever to hit the ground.

And then the lizard brain kicked in.

Fear! Trapped! Run! Run! Rruunrunrun!

Go to the light! I ordered my new body. But the body was afraid of the light. It was terrified.

Go to the light! I screamed inside my head. And suddenly I was there.

In the bright light I realised how bad the lizard eyes were. I couldn't make sense of what I was seeing. Everything was shattered and twisted around. Down was up and up was down.

K A Applegate

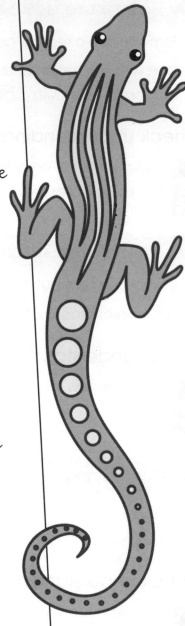

Chat challenge

Who is telling the story?
Who is the story about?
Are they the same person?
Does the character have a name or not?
Which word tells you who is telling the story?
Does it make the story more interesting or not? Give some reasons.
How is the lizard's view of the world different from the narrator?

Comprehension

1) How do you know from the first line when the story starts and where it is set?

2) What is **morphing**? Look in a dictionary to find out more about the prefix of the word and its meaning.

3) What does the author change into?

4) What is DNA? Do some research to find out how this helps the narrator to morph.

5) When the process of changing begins, what does the narrator liken it to?

6) How does the layout of the writing help you to know how the character thinks as a lizard?

7) Why did the character find it difficult to go to the light?

Objective focus

1) Is the narrator a character in the story? Whose point of view are we being given in the story? Identify the words that tell us.

2) A first-person narrator (**I**) allows us to see directly into the head of the character. If this is the case, how much can the character describe in detail at any one time? Can you find examples of this in the text? How much detail is there? How much does the writing appeal to our senses?

3) First-person narrators show us the story through one viewpoint. Is this more or less exciting? Do you sympathise more or less with the character? Find any examples in the text to prove what you say.

4) Can you see any drawbacks to using a first-person narrator when telling a story? For example, are you limited to times and places? How much of what they are telling you can you believe?

Links to writing

1) Continue with the story in the first person. How does it feel to be a lizard? What does he do?

   Try to avoid using 'I' all the time at the beginning of sentences.
   Include as much detail as seems right for the character in that situation.
   Use short paragraphs as you change from one subject or event to another.
   This will increase the tension.

2) Tell the same story from Cassie's point of view in the first person. Use the same features. Does she see or feel the same things? Compare the two versions.

15 Narrative techniques – third person

From *Warrior Scarlet*

This book is set in the Bronze age – over a thousand years ago. Drem is a boy whose arm is crippled. Here he is on a wolf hunt.

And suddenly the wolf was there. With a crashing of twigs and small branches it sprang into the open, then, seeing the hunters all about it, checked almost in mid-spring, swinging its head from side to side, with laid-back ears and wrinkled muzzle: a great, brindled dog wolf, menace in every raised hackle. Then, as though it knew with which of the hunters it had to deal, as though it expected him, it looked full at Drem. For a long moment it stood there, tensed to spring, savage amber eyes on his as though it knew and greeted him. The rest of the band had checked at a small distance, spears ready; but Drem was no longer aware of them; only of the wolf, his wolf.

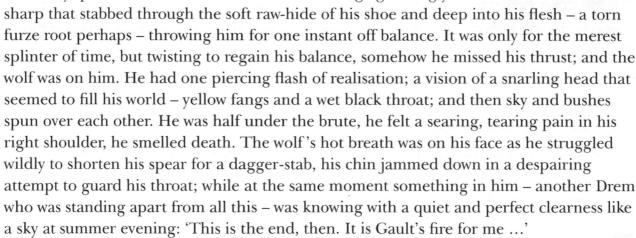

…

It seemed to him that the open jaws with their lolling tongue were grinning at him as he leapt forward and ran in low, his spear drawn back to strike. And at the same instant the wolf sprang.

Quite what happened he never knew; it was all so quick, so hideously quick. His foot came down on something agonisingly sharp that stabbed through the soft raw-hide of his shoe and deep into his flesh – a torn furze root perhaps – throwing him for one instant off balance. It was only for the merest splinter of time, but twisting to regain his balance, somehow he missed his thrust; and the wolf was on him. He had one piercing flash of realisation; a vision of a snarling head that seemed to fill his world – yellow fangs and a wet black throat; and then sky and bushes spun over each other. He was half under the brute, he felt a searing, tearing pain in his right shoulder, he smelled death. The wolf's hot breath was on his face as he struggled wildly to shorten his spear for a dagger-stab, his chin jammed down in a despairing attempt to guard his throat; while at the same moment something in him – another Drem who was standing apart from all this – was knowing with a quiet and perfect clearness like a sky at summer evening: 'This is the end, then. It is Gault's fire for me …'

Rosemary Sutcliff

Chat challenge

Who is telling the story? How do you know?
Who is the story about?
Are they the same person?
Does the character have a name or not?
How is this way of telling a story different from a first-person narrator, e.g. someone who starts a story, 'I … '?
Does having a narrator like this make the story different? Give some reasons.

English Study Guide: Year 6

Answer Booklet

1 Spelling strategies – *i before e*
Comprehension
1) conceited
2) heir
3) grieve, achieve, perceive, receive, deceive, believe
4) seize, weird, heir, protein
5) *Own answer*
6) heir, friend

Objective focus
1) a. friend
   b. thief
   c. quiet
   d. height
2) a. believe
   b. yield
   c. grief
   d. receive
   e. conceive
   f. piece
   g. relief
   h. receipt
3) *I* before *ie* in *believe*
   y before *ie* in *yield*
   r before *ie* in *grief*
   c before *ei* in *conceive*
   p before *ie* in *piece*
   c before *ei* in *receipt*
   The rule does work.
4) *Own answer*

Links to writing
1) re-lief
   de-ceit-ful
   brief
   pro-tein
   yield
   re-ceive
   piece
   niece
   heir
   siege
2) mischief
   deceitful
   receipt
   deceit
   receive
   deceive
3) *Own answer*

2 Spelling strategies – derivation
Comprehension
1) news
   alphabet
   caravan
   junk
   gaffer (**Old** English)
2) wellington
   far-fetched
3) a. macIntosh
   b. sandwich
   c. teddy
4) no
5) People travelled around the world visiting other countries, selling and trading goods. They took their language with them.

Objective focus
1) An etymological dictionary explains the origin of words as well as their meanings.
2) a. *un-* from the Latin *unicus* meaning 'one', **unique** means 'being the only one'.
   b. *tri-* from Latin and Greek meaning 'three'; **triangle** means 'a polygon having three sides'.
   c. *deci-* from Latin meaning 'tith' or 10; **decimal** means 'based on the number 10'.

d. *oct-* from Latin meaning 'eight'; **octet** means 'a group or set of eight'.
   e. *bi-* from Latin meaning 'two'; **biscuit** means 'twice baked'.
3) a. Greece
   b. America
   c. Germany

Links to writing
1), 2) *Own answers*

3 Mnemonics
Comprehension
1) *Own answer*
2) principal/principle
   there/their
   separate
   dessert/desert
3) Concentrate on the letters of the words:
   arithmetic
   necessary
   rhythm
   Mississippi
   Concentrate on the sounds of the words:
   their/there
   principal/principle
   dessert/desert
4), 5) *Own answers*

Objective focus
1) a. dangerous
   b. piece
   c. chocolate
2), 3) *Own answers*

Links to writing
1), 2), 3) *Own answers*

4 Editing, proofreading
Comprehension
1) *Own answer*
2) Poet tree = poetry
   mist aches = mistakes
   chequer = checker
   pea sea = pc
   marquees = marks
   four = for
   revue = review
   miss steaks = mistakes
   eye = i
   sea = see
   quay = key
   right = write
   weight = wait
   two = to
   weather = whether
   oar = or
   write = right
   strait = straight
   maid = made
   nose = knows
   bee fore = before
   to = too
   putt = put
   rite = right
   rarely = really
   threw = through
   shore = sure
   your = you're
   too = to
   no = know
   weigh = way
   tolled = told
   sew = so
   sauce = source
3), 4), 5) *Own answers*

Objective focus
1) Any ten from: chequer, revue, sea, eye, quay, right, weight, oar, strait, maid, pea sea, four, marquees, miss steaks, two, weather, write, nose, bee fore, to, putt, rite, rarely, threw, shore, your, too, no, weigh, tolled, sew
2) a. eight
   b. saw
   c. steal
   d. tale
   e. too/to
   f. their
   g. bare
   h. pore/paw
   i. reign
   j. for
3) a. Large tents set up for an outdoor gathering.
   b. A structure built on the bank of a waterway for use as a landing place.
   c. A golf stroke made on a putting green causing the ball to roll into the hole.
   d. A ceremonial act or action.
   e. To toll is to sound a bell by pulling a rope. (multiple definitions possible)
4) Homophones: words which sound the same but have different spelling and meanings.
   Homonyms: words which are spelled the same and pronounced the same but have different meanings.
   Homographs: words spelled the same but have different meaning or pronunciations.

Links to writing
1), 2), 3), 4) *Own answers*

6 Point of view
Comprehension
1) The fire fighters would see very little because they are behind their fire engine.
   The journalist with the camera would see only the back of the red car.
   The police officer would see more than the journalist with the camera, although his view is still mainly from behind the accident.
   The character in the green shirt and blue trousers would see the front of the red car.
   The driver of the lorry is higher up, so would see the front of the red car and all around him.
   The driver of the red car would see the front of the lorry from very close up, but not much else.
   The passenger in the back would see the back of the driver's head.
   The girl, the boy on crutches, the girl holding his hand and the boy in the green shirt and orange trousers have the best view of the accident; they can see the lorry and the car from the side.
   The man in blue coming from the helicopter would see the red car from behind.
2) Yes
3) The fire fighters would only hear and, possibly, smell the accident.
   The drivers and passenger would hear, see, feel and smell the accident.
   All the other characters would see, hear and smell the accident.
4) None of the people at the accident will actually know the whole truth. Everybody would have a different viewpoint depending on where they are and how they are involved. For example, while the driver of the lorry may have seen the whole event, he may be worried about being blamed and tell lies.
5) Each person will tell the story of the accident differently. Those directly involved in the accident (drivers, passenger) and those witnessing the accident taking place

(bystanders) will use the first person. Those arriving on the scene after the accident (police officer, journalist) will use the third person so that their reports will seem more balanced.

Objective focus
1), 2), 3), 4), 5) *Own answers*

Links to writing
1), 2) *Own answers*

7 Structures
Comprehension
1) The first paragraph describes the author's part of East London.
2) 'My part of East London has a character all its own' is the topic sentence and the rest of the paragraph develops the idea using details.
3) Paragraph two describes the railway arches. Paragraph three describes one particular railway arch.
4) The focus moves from East London then to the Docklands Light Railway then the text focuses on the railway arches. The author finishes by describing one particular railway arch.
5) The text is a story because it is written in the present tense and describes a place rather than a person.

Objective focus
1) *Own answer*
2) Speech is set out in paragraphs because it is easier to understand who says what. If speech is not in paragraphs the reader may get confused. Remember: New speaker, new line.

Links to writing
1), 2), 3) *Own answers*

8 Changing word meanings in different contexts
Comprehension
1) The bony upper portion of a nose. When it refers to a structure over an obstacle, like a river or road.
2) The top part of a head. When it refers to what a king or queen wears on their head.
3) A thin membrane that receives sound inside an ear.
4) *Own answer*

Objective focus
1) a. The woman pined for her lost love.
   It was the tallest pine in the forest.
   b. A bird was hiding in the rushes.
   Don't rush in the corridor.
   c. The farmer ploughed his field.
   Biology was her chosen field.
   d. The prince went to the ball.
   The princess caught the ball.
   e. To start the fire, strike the match.
   Liverpool has won the match!
2) a. She climbed over the rock.
   He only listened to rock and roll.
   b. The family looked at the old picture album.
   The band had the number one album in the country.
   c. You can hold paper together with a rubber band.
   The band had the number one album in the country.
   d. The lid came off with a pop.
   Kylie was Henry's favourite pop star.
3) a. I shot the sheriff.
   The film was shot on location in the Wild West.
   b. I will still be here at the end of the day.
   Umair used a still from his favourite movie in a presentation.
   c. A film of dust settled on the furniture.
   Micah's favourite film is *Star Wars*.
   d. Use this map to find our location.
   The film was shot on location in the Wild West.
4) a. I am the most popular person at school.
   Populous means 'densely populated'.
   b. The River Nile irrigates the land every year.
   Irritates means 'to provoke anger or displeasure'.
   c. I speak properly. I've taken elocution lessons.
   Electrocution means 'to kill by electric shock'.

Links to writing
1), 2) *Own answers*

9 Devices to argue and persuade
Comprehension
1) People play competitive sports to win.
2) The author says it creates hatred, jealousy and boastfulness.
3) *Own answer*
4) He blames the spectators.
5) The author writes that spectators cheer their own side and boo the opposition.

Objective focus
1) 'You play to win, and the game has little meaning unless you do your utmost to win'. Yes, speaking to the reader using **you** is more persuasive than using I.
2) 'Anyone who has played in a school football match knows this.' 'People want to see one side on top and the other side humiliated'.
3) These words signal to the reader that another argument is about to be made, focusing the reader's attention on the new argument.
4) '... are not the most savage combative instincts aroused?' Instead of presenting the argument, it brings the reader into the argument making them think about the issue personally.

Links to writing
1) *Own answer*

10 Cool reads
Comprehension
1) The book is about a boy who loves football.
2) Every book in the world has a unique number to identify it. With this number anyone wanting to read the book can find it easily.
3) The game between the Panthers and the Swifts is the most exciting part of the book.
4) Luke isn't good at football, but knows everything there is to know about the sport.
5) The writer says this because the reader might not expect Luke's team to win because he is not good at football.
6) The book is in chapters and is not too long.

Objective focus
1) The storyline is easy to follow. Luke has never played football for this school before, but as the flu virus hits the school he finally gets his chance to play. However, it doesn't go well. His captain, Matthew, is always putting Luke down, but Luke just ignores him. Soon, Luke's Sunday team The Swifts draws with Matthew's Sunday team The Panthers. The game is the most exciting part of the book and, believe it or not, Luke's team wins.
2) *Own answer*
3) Luke's team wins. There is only one team, Luke's, and verb ending should agree with this.
4) Soccer at Sandford, Sandford on Tour, The Big Match, The Big Day, The Big Goal, The Big Kick, The Big Game, The Big Prize, The Big Chance, The Big Star, The Big Hit, The Big Freeze, The Big Break, All Goalies are Crazy, Football Daft, Football Flukes
5) *Own answer*

Links to writing
1), 2) *Own answers*

11 Writers from different times
Comprehension
1) The reader can recognise faces, clothing and the characters' names are used.
2) Romeo is the hero and Juliet is the heroine. The reader knows this because they are the main focus of the cartoon and they end up kissing.
3) How the characters interact, stand in relation to one another and their facial expressions.
4) No, the cartoon uses simplified English to aid understanding. There is less space in cartoons.
5) Names of the characters appear in bold and the reader is given a stage direction.
6) What the characters say to one another tells us how the characters should react to each other. For example, Juliet says 'Come hither nurse' which tells us that the nurse is her servant.
7) It is not necessary to use playscript features in the cartoon because the reader can see the characters. Speech bubbles are used instead of characters' names in bold.

Objective focus
1) a. Your mother wants to speak with you.
   b. Her mother is the most important woman in the house.
   c. Get over here, nurse.
   d. Who's that man over there?
2) a. foolish or stupid
   b. a peasant
   c. deeply respectful
   d. abrasive
   e. poor or needy
3) *Own answer*

Links to writing
1) *Own answer*

12 Writers from different places
Comprehension
1) The place they lived was remote and not many people lived there.
2) They knew there were many houses, candy and calico and other wonderful things.
3) Their father would trade furs in the stores.
4) The snow and icicles tell you that it is winter.
5) Lighting the way and helping to milk the cow.
6) They were surprised because Sukey normally lived in the barn at that time of year.

Objective focus
1), 2) *Own answers*

Links to writing
1) *Own answer*

14 Narrative techniques – first person
Comprehension
1) The first line says 'I did it Monday morning in my locker at school.'
2) Morphing means 'to undergo a transformation'. The prefix **morph-** means 'form'.
3) The author changes into a lizard.
4) DNA is the basic instructions that tell each of your cells what to do. If the narrator has the DNA from a lizard, his cells have all the information they need to change.
5) He likens it to falling off a skyscraper and taking forever to hit the ground.
6) The layout changes to single sentences with exclamation marks, which is more basic than the previous text.
7) The character finds it difficult to go to the light because the lizard part of him is afraid of it.

Objective focus
1) Yes, the narrator is a character in the story. We are being given the story in the first person. The words that tell us this are **I** and **we**.
2) The character can describe in some detail, but is limited to describing what they alone experience, for example: 'It had been fairly creepy,' and 'It was like falling.' The descriptions are all linked to the senses. Experiences of touch, sight and sound are all described.
3) The first person can be more exciting than the third person. We are encouraged to sympathise more closely with the character because they seem to speak directly to us. 'I did it on Monday morning in my locker at school' sounds like the confession of a secret.
4) First-person narration limits you to one person's experience. It is also potentially biased.

Links to writing
1), 2) *Own answers*

15 Narrative techniques – third person
Comprehension
1) Drem knew the wolf was there because of the crashing of twigs and small branches.
2) The wolf swung its head from side to side, laid back its ears and had a wrinkled muzzle.
3) His foot came down on something sharp, stabbing through his shoe.
4) Drem didn't throw his spear because when he was regaining his balance the wolf sprang too close.
5) Drem's impression of the wolf was of a snarling head that seemed to fill his world – yellow fangs and a wet black throat.
6) The wolf injured him by hurting his right shoulder.

Objective focus
1) No, the narrator is not a character in the story, which is being told in the third person. We are

being given the narrator's point of view about the scene and Drem. The words that tell the reader this are it and him/his/he.

2) If you were being attacked by a wolf, you would not be able to describe all the details that are given here.

3) The narrator describes the gruesome appearance of the wolf and Drem's painful experience of stabbing his foot.

4) Quite what happened I never knew; it was all so quick, so hideously quick. My foot came down on something agonisingly sharp that stabbed through the soft raw-hide of my shoe and deep into my flesh – a torn furze root perhaps – throwing me for one instant off balance. It was only for the merest splinter of time, but twisting to regain my balance, somehow I missed my thrust; and the wolf was on me. I had one piercing flash of realisation; a vision of a snarling head that seemed to fill my world – yellow fangs and a wet black throat; and then sky and bushes spun over each other. I was half under the brute, I felt a searing, tearing pain in my right shoulder, I smelled death. The wolf's hot breath was on my face as I struggled wildly to shorten my spear for a dagger-stab, my chin jammed down in a despairing attempt to guard my throat; while at the same moment something in me – another Drem who was standing apart from all this – was knowing with a quiet and perfect calmness like a sky at summer evening: 'This is the end, then. It is Gault's fire for me …'

Realistically, a first-person narrator would not be able to give this much detail if they were being attacked in this way. The third person is more exciting here because the details help to build tension and paint a dramatic picture of the scene.

Links to writing
1) *Own answer*

16 Formal and informal writing: instructional
Comprehension
1) A solute is a solid that dissolves in a liquid or solvent.
2) Baking soda.
3) The writing is set out in three sections, with each having a title. The first section gives background, the second tells the reader what materials they will need and the third section tells the reader how to do the experiment.
4) The writer uses numbers to clearly identify the different stages of the experiment.
5) Some words are in brackets in the materials and procedure section to give additional information, options or give a chemical's everyday name.

Objective focus
1) *Own answer*
   The purpose of the text changes from inform to describe and the audience becomes somebody the writer knows rather than a stranger. Rewriting the instructions informally makes them more difficult to understand and follow because important information is lost in unnecessary details.
2) They use this type of writing because they want to make instructions as easy to understand as possible in case people have to read it quickly.
   a. A blow-up raft for babies is available if you need one.
   b. To keep safe do what all the signs tell you to do.
   c. Press this button to get a crew member if you need help.
3) *Own answer*

Links to writing
1), 2), 3) *Own answers*

17 Formal and informal writing: biography
Comprehension
1) You know that Hannah was Jewish because she attended Hebrew school and synagogue.
2) Hannah was gangly, tall, had creamy skin, brown hair and soft, brown eyes.
3) The central character in the biography is the main focus of the text, so it is important to know

what they look like.
4) Her friend Anne was outspoken, impudent, and loved having fun.
5) Hannah was more interested in lessons while Anne was more interested in socialising and boyfriends.
6) Life is no longer simple for them because of the war and them being thirteen.
7) It was shocking that a law was passed so Jews were forbidden from working in most professions. It seems wrong that someone shouldn't be allowed to work because of their religion.

Objective focus
1)

Feature	Evidence from text
Third person	*'She went to Hebrew school two times a week and to synagogue.'*
Personal details	*'She was gangly, tall and had creamy skin.'*
Past or present tense	*'Anne was outspoken …'*
Chronological structure	*'At age thirteen, this morning, lately, no longer'*
Informal or formal language	*'The differences between Hannah and Anne had become more pronounced.'*

2) *Own answer*

Links to writing
1) *Own answer*

18 Organising texts: diaries
Comprehension
1) Sarajevo is the capital of Bosnia and Herzegovina, which is located near the Adriatic Sea. After the break-up of Yugoslavia, many sides fought for power in the region.
2) A diary is set up by date, with events from the day discussed in the first person.
3) Zlata is talking to her diary.
4) She complains about being bored and the monotony of her life.
5) She dreams about her idol Michael Jackson and not being able to get his autograph. *Own answer*
6) Yes, the war seems very important to miss out of her diary.

Objective focus
1)

Feature	Evidence from text
First person	*'I really do have to go to bed now!'*
Personal details	*'Everything is the same and keeps going in a circle (in my holiday life). Boredom, books, friends, phone calls and so on.'*
Past or present tense	*'We saw M&M and Needa off.'* *'I'm off to bed now.'*
Chronological order of events	*'Monday, 13 January 1992'* *'Tuesday, 14 January 1992'*
Formal or informal	*'Sad. Poor me. Ha, ha, ha…'*

2) Different tenses are used because the diary recounts things that happened in the past and also how the writer is feeling at the time of writing.

Links to writing
1), 2) *Own answers*

19 Paragraphs
Comprehension
1) She was alone in the house because her father had gone to London.
2) It is important to know that her father was far away to emphasise how alone she was.
3) She looked in her wardrobe and under her bed to make sure that nobody or nothing was hiding.
4) This tells us that she is nervous about being alone.
5) The last line is a shock because we expect the room to be empty.
6) No, not identifying the voice makes it scarier.

Objective focus
1) The writer uses these paragraphs because they are different topics.

Paragraph	Subject – what happens
1	We learn she is alone
2	She secures her bedroom
3	She dresses for bed
4	She gets into bed, turns off light
5	A voice speaks

The writer uses these paragraphs to mark clearly the different things that the girl does as she prepares to sleep.
2) *Own answer*
   Holding back important information until the end of the paragraph builds suspense.

Links to writing
1), 2) *Own answers*

21 Argument – using sentences to persuade
Comprehension
1) 120,000
2) Over 400 chemicals, including tar, carbon monoxide and nicotine.
3) Lung cancer and heart disease.
4) Passive smoking is breathing in other people's cigarette smoke.
5) The writer wants a ban on smoking.
6) *Own answer*

Objective focus
1) The passage becomes more like an information text which states facts, rather than a persuasive text.
2) Statement of fact: *'Smoking causes 120,000 death in the UK each year.'*
   Using contrast: *'Surely you cannot deny the fact that smoking cigarettes increases the chance of suffering a heart attack by two to three times compared to a non-smoker?'*
   Using cause and effect: *'If we stopped it now, we would save 330 lives per day.'*
   Using conditional language: *'we should leave them to smoke if they want to.'*
   Using repetition: *'so I say it again: …passive smoking is dangerous.'*
   Using rhetorical questions: *'Surely you cannot deny the fact that smoking cigarettes increases the chance of suffering a heart attack by two to three times compared to a non-smoker?'*
   Using personal language: *'you cannot deny'.*
3) *Own answer*

Links to writing
1) Statement of fact provides proof.
   Using contrast shows both sides of an argument.
   Using cause and effect demonstrates the consequences of a particular action.
   Using conditional language allows the writer to make opinions sound like facts.
   Using repetition emphasises a key point.
   Using a rhetorical question makes the answer to a question sound obvious.
   Personal language helps the writer form a closer relationship with the reader.
2) *Own answer*

22 Constructing sentences in varied ways 1
Comprehension
1) Winter
2) **Confections** mean 'any type of sweet foods'. The frost on the trees remind the author of sweets covered with sugar.
3) Sight: *'Sparkling and motionless'*
   Smell: *'Smelled like needles'*
   Hearing: *'Solid sound'*
   Taste: *'Confections of sugar'*
4) The dog reminded him of a ghost in a cloud because the dog's breath was warm and producing a cloud of vapour.
5) He describes the boys as *'wrapped like Russians'* to make us realise how cold it is and how many clothes they are wearing.
6) They have multi-coloured noses because some have gone blue from the cold while others have gone red.
7) The author really means everything was covered with ice and was still.

Objective focus

1) Simile: *'A dog trotted past like a ghost in a cloud.'*
   Metaphor: *'Everything was rigid, locked-up and sealed.'*
2) **a.** A few minutes earlier
   b. When at last we reached
   c. Peering through the window
3) *Own answer*

Links to writing

1) *Own answer*

23 Constructing sentences in varied ways 2
Comprehension

1) Bits of string and catnip.
2) Cats only play with special cat toys – their owners. They only play to please us.
3) Cat food can come out of tins. Cats cannot open tins – they need an opener. Hence they would see their owners as performing this important function.
4) Owners feel sorry for them and feel guilty so they feed them more.
5) Mouse, frog, feathers. They will be messy: 'bits of …'.
6) Sitting on mats, clean washing, steps in front of you and your comfortable chair in the garden.
7) We are supposed to own the cat but they have such power over us that the author suggests it is the other way around.

Objective focus

1), 2), 3), 4), 5) *Own answers*

Links to writing

1), 2), 3) *Own answers*

24 Colons or semicolons
Comprehension

1) As the desert was neither flat nor monotonous it was not like other ones.
2) The colours of the desert were strong: bold and harsh and sharply defined …: *'belts of yellow, block of bottle-green, patches of fire flame-red, and fields of blood.'*
3) When she first saw the aboriginal boy her first reaction was to grab Peter and run, but the boy's appearance stopped her from doing this.
4) Peter
5) She notices that he has black skin with a hint of under-surface bronze and that it is fine-grained: glossy, satiny, almost silk-like. His hair was not crinkly but nearly straight.
6) In his hand was a baby rock wallaby.

Objective focus

1) *'And its colours were strong: bold and harsh and sharply defined.'*
2) *Own answer*
3) **a.** The enemy was advancing: defeat was certain.
   b. He left really pleased with himself: everything was going well in his life.
4) *'The girl's first impulse was to grab Peter and run; but as her eyes swept over the stranger, her fear died slowly away.'*

Links to writing

1), 2), 3) *Own answers*

25 Dashes or brackets
Comprehension

1) Mr Jingle's luggage consisted of a brown paper parcel.
2) Mr Jingle says that the rest of his luggage has already been sent ahead 'by water', meaning by boat.
3) He is trying to make himself seem more important than he is by describing to the coachman the heavy and awkward luggage that has already been sent ahead. It is hard to believe him because all he seems to own is a shirt and a handkerchief.
4) He tells people to take care of their heads because the coach is about to pass under a low archway.
5) He tells how a tall woman had her head knocked off while eating sandwiches when she passed under the arch the other day.
6) The story is comic.
7) Mr Jingle likes to tell a good story and to shock people. He doesn't care about the truth of the story just so long as he can amaze his listeners.

Objective focus

1) 'Heads, heads, take care of your heads,' cried the stranger, as they came out under the low archway, which in those days formed the entrance to the coach-yard. 'This is a terrible and dangerous place. The other day, five children were travelling on this same coach with their mother. The mother was a tall lady, and as she sat here eating sandwiches she forgot about the low arch. The children heard a crash and a knock, looked around and saw their mother with her sandwich still in her hand, but no mouth to put it in. Her head had been completely taken off. Isn't that shocking?'
   This sounds less like spontaneous speech and more like a rehearsed recount. The story is less funny this way and we don't get a sense of Mr Jingle's distinctive, jerky way of speaking.
2) *Own answer*
3) I wanted to become a gospel singer (I had always sung gospel music with my father – he used to sing back home in Jamaica) so I joined a choir in south London.

Links to writing

1), 2), 3) *Own answers*

26 Punctuation clarifying meaning
Comprehension

1) If the punctuation is changed, the meaning of the sentences changes also.
2) When spoken the sentences could all sound exactly the same.
3) Emphasis is important to make meaning clear. E.g. 'You will be required to work **twenty** four hour shifts' means twenty shifts of four hours each. 'You will be required to work **twenty-four-hour** shifts' means that each shift will be 24 hours long.
4) Different punctuation can change the meaning of a sentence in unexpected and amusing ways. *'When I sing well, ladies feel sick'* means if he does a good job at singing then ladies will feel ill. *'When I sing, well ladies feel sick.'* means no matter how he sings, healthy ladies in the audience will feel ill.

Objective focus

1) **a.** Listen to the hot-water tap in the sink. / The sound of hot-water tapping in the sink. Turn off the hot-water-tap. / Stop the flow of water from the hot-water-tap.
   b. Where is the stack of fifty dollar-notes? (50 $1 notes) / I have never seen fifty-dollar-notes before. ($50 notes)
   c. He is a grand-piano salesman. (He sells grand-pianos.) / He is a grand piano-salesman. (He is good at selling pianos.)
2) **a.** We order, merchandise and sell the products. (A list of three things they do.) / We order merchandise, and sell the products. (Two things they do.)
   b. Have your car serviced today! Free oil included. (We encourage you to get your car serviced today, but oil is always included free in the service.) / Have your car serviced! Today, free oil included. (Only today, you get free oil with your service.)
   c. I shall buy a car, in part-exchange, for my wife. (He is purchasing a car by exchanging his wife for part of the value of the new vehicle.) / I shall buy a car in part-exchange, for my wife. (He is purchasing a new car for his wife, by exchanging an old one.)
   d. 'The teachers,' said Emma 'should be quiet.' (Emma thinks the teachers should not make noise.) / The teachers said, 'Emma should be quiet'. (The teachers think Emma should not make noise.)
   e. We give quality service, and attention to detail. (The service is quality and they also pay attention to detail.) / We give quality, service and attention to detail. (A list of three things they do.)

Links to writing

1) **a.** DANGER! NO SKATING ALLOWED. / DANGER? NO. SKATING ALLOWED!
   b. 'Come and eat Fred,' said mum. / 'Come and eat, Fred!' said mum.
   c. 'Can you see Fred?' called Max through the fog. / 'Can you see, Fred?' called Max through the fog.
   d. Don't use commas, which are not necessary. / Don't! Use commas which are not necessary.
2) *Own answer*

27 Speech
Comprehension

1) A mother, father and their son Chas are in conversation. We are told that the father is speaking in the second paragraph and the mother's reaction to what he says is also given. Chas asks if he can go and see the old laundry.
2) The mother talks about the 'dive bomber' and the 'shelter' in the first paragraph.
3) Chas is keen to have a look at the crashed plane because his father's description makes the crash and explosion seem massive.
4) They let him go because he won't find anything but bricks; everything else has been destroyed.
5) 'gonner' instead of **dead**
   'nowt' instead of **nothing**
   'cos' instead of **because**
   'me face' instead of **my face**
   'D'you' instead of **Do you**
6) Non-standard English in speech is permitted because it recreates the natural or distinctive way in which people speak.

Objective focus

1) By constantly saying who is speaking we lose the sense that this is natural speech. The writing becomes repetitive and slow. New speaker, new line makes it obvious who is speaking anyway.
2), 3) *Own answers*
4) If we are told how the characters look then we are able to understand how they feel and therefore how they are likely to speak. *Own answer*

Links to writing

1), 2) *Own answers*

Author: Andrew Plaistowe
Design: Clive Sutherland
Editorial: Dodi Beardshaw

Comprehension

1) How did Drem know that the wolf was there?

2) What kind of things did the wolf do when it knew that it was trapped?

3) What happened to make Drem fall?

4) Why didn't Drem throw his spear?

5) What was Drem's impression of the wolf when it attacked him?

6) How did the wolf injure Drem?

Objective focus

1) Is the narrator a character in the story? Whose point of view are we being given in the story? Identify the words that tell us.

2) A third-person narrator can explain what is going on around the character in a lot more detail than a first-person narrator. Find examples of this in the third paragraph. For example, if you were being attacked by a wolf, how much of this would you be able to describe at the moment?

3) Third-person narrators are often better for explaining the internal thoughts and feelings of a character in a tense situation. Find examples of how the description appeals to our senses in the passage, so we get a sense of how the character feels.

4) Why is this level of explanation difficult if you are using the first person **I** form? Rewrite the third paragraph using the first person, the **I** form. What difference does this make if any to the excitement of the description?

Links to writing

1) What happens next? Plan the rest of the story. How is Drem rescued? What happens at the end?

   As you write your story, try to:
   ● **show how Drem feels**
   ● **interweave detail about the setting as you write**
   ● **use a variety of sentence structures – some short and some complex – for dramatic effect**
   ● **find ways to avoid repeating words**
   ● **use a variety of punctuation (e.g.** semicolons**) to break up longer sentences.**

16 Formal and informal writing: instructional

To grow crystals from a supersaturated solution

A solid that dissolves in a liquid or **solvent** is called a **solute**.

Materials

2 tall narrow jars	spoon	magnifying glass	magnesium sulphate (Epsom salts)
tweezers	thread	sugar	
kettle	washer or paperclip (optional)	sodium chloride (salt)	sodium bicarbonate (baking soda)
rubber band			
pencil	coffee filter papers		

Procedure

This experiment will take a few days to complete. If you are having difficulty forming crystals, try tying a small washer or paperclip to the end of the string.

Fill one jar with hot water and stir in one of the salts until no more salt will dissolve.

1 Tie one end of the thread to the middle of a pencil and carefully hang the thread in the solution so it is not touching the bottom or the sides.

2 When no more crystals have grown on the thread, remove and place it on a coffee filter.

3 Pour the liquid into a second jar, being careful not to pour out any crystals.

4 Carefully scrape the crystals off the thread (or remove any off the bottom of the jar) and examine them using a magnifying glass.

5 If large enough single crystals are formed, tie one to some thread and hang it in the saved saturated solution to see if it grows over the following days.

Chat challenge

What is the purpose of this piece of writing?
Who is it aimed at?
Would you describe the writing as formal or informal? Explain why.

Comprehension

1) What is a solute?

2) What is another name for sodium bicarbonate?

3) How is the writing set out to make reading and understanding easier?

4) Why does the writer use numbers in explaining the procedure?

5) Why are some words in brackets in the materials section and in the procedure section?

Objective focus

1) Rewrite part of the experiment informally, e.g. 'We took some absolutely boiling water, put in lovely white salt and gave it a stir.' What differences to the purpose and audience would this make? Why is this not appropriate to a science experiment?

2) Here are some examples of formal language found on a plane. Why do they use such language? Write the expressions in everyday language.

Infant flotation devices available.

For your safety you must comply with all signs.

Press button to summon crew member if assistance is required.

3) Write two descriptions: a tree trunk and a flower. The first description is for a science lesson and the second will appear in a story. How will they be different? Consider your audience.

Links to writing

1) Write a set of instructions in formal English that you would find in a box when you buy a new product, e.g. how to play a DVD.

2) Write the same instructions in a letter to a friend, starting: 'I bought a new DVD player the other day. It was dead easy to use. All you do is …'

3) Use a computer to produce both types of writing described in questions 1 and 2 as they would normally be seen. Display them side by side and highlight:

the differences in formal and informal language

the suitability for the purpose of the writing

the suitability for each different audience.

17 Formal and informal writing: biography

From *Hannah Goslar Remembers*

At age thirteen Hannah Goslar was fun-loving but also quite religious. She went to Hebrew school two times a week and to synagogue. She was gangly, tall, had creamy skin, and brushed her mahogany brown hair so fast that electric sparks crackled. Hannah's best features were her soft, brown eyes.

This morning she was going to call for her friend, Anne Frank. Anne was outspoken, even impudent; she loved having fun. She was more interested in socialising and boyfriends than Hebrew lessons. Lately the differences between Hannah and Anne had become more pronounced. With the war raging and both of them being thirteen, life was not as simple as it used to be when they were little girls sitting side by side in school.

Hannah had kissed her father before she left the house. Because of a new law that Jews were forbidden from working in most professions, Mr Goslar was no longer allowed to work as a professional economist. This meant that it was difficult for him to support his family.

Alison Leslie Gold

Chat challenge

Who is this passage about?

Who is the narrator? Is it the same person?

What is the purpose of this kind of writing?

What kind of information does it give?

Is the historical background important?

Which tense is it written in?

Would you say this text is formal or informal in its style?

Why do you think people write biographies of some people but not of others? Find examples of biographies in the library to see if you can reach a conclusion.

Comprehension

1) How do you know what religion Hannah followed?

2) What did Hannah look like?

3) Why is it important to be able to imagine what characters look like in biographies?

4) What was Hannah's friend Anne like?

5) What were some of the differences between Hannah and Anne?

6) Why was life no longer so simple for Hannah and Anne?

7) Do you find anything shocking in the third paragraph? Explain carefully.

Objective focus

1) Complete a chart with evidence to show some features of biography:

Feature	Evidence from text
Third person	
Personal details	
Past or present tense	
Chronological structure	
Informal or formal language	

2) Find out more about Anne Frank. You could use the Internet or read her diary. How will you decide which are the most important pieces of information to use? Plan and write the first chapter of a biography of Anne Frank using the features discussed and identified in your work here.

Links to writing

1) Research and write the biography of someone you admire.

Use books and the Internet to research.

Write notes and then sort them into the facts you will use. A flow chart may help.

How will you structure the biography?

Will you start at the beginning of their lives and move in chronological order?

Will you start at the person's death and move backwards?

18 Organising texts: diaries

From *Zlata's Diary: A Child's Life in Sarajevo*

Zlata lived in Sarajevo in the early 1990s when there was a war.

Diary

Monday, 13 January 1992

We saw M&M and Needa off. AUHHHH! It's been a long day! I'm off to bed now – it's 23.10. I'm reading *Captain at Fift*een by Jules Verne.

Everything is the same and keeps going in a circle (in my holiday life). Boredom, books, friends, phone calls and so on. I really do have to go to bed now! GOOD NIGHT AND SWEET DREAMS!

Tuesday, 14 January 1992

I yawned, opened my pen and started to write: I'm listening to music from Top Gun on 'Good Vibrations' [on the radio]. Something else is on now. I've just destroyed the back page of *Bazar* [a fashion magazine]. I talked to Mummy on the phone. She's at work.

I have something to tell you. Every night I dream that I'm asking Michael Jackson for his autograph, but either he won't give it to me or his secretary writes it, and then all the letters melt, because Michael Jackson didn't write them. Sad. Poor me. Ha, ha, ha …

Zlata Filipovic

Chat challenge

Who is this passage about?
Who is the narrator? Is it the same person?
What is the purpose of this kind of writing?
What kind of information does it give?
Is the historical background important?
Which tense is it written in?
Would you say this was formal or informal in its style? Why?

Comprehension

1) Where is Sarajevo and why was there a war there? Look in an atlas or on the Internet to find out.

2) How is a diary set out?

3) Who is Zlata 'talking' to in her diary?

4) What does Zlata complain about? Do you complain about the same things?

5) What does Zlata dream about? Do you dream about the same kind of things?

6) Does it surprise you that Zlata does not write about the war? Why?

Objective focus

1) Complete a chart with evidence to show the features of a diary:

Feature	Evidence from text
First person	
Personal details	
Past and present tense	
Chronological order of events	
Formal or informal language	

2) Why are different tenses used in the diary?

Links to writing

1) After reading a book, pick a character that you would like to be. Write down a list of their characteristics, especially paying close attention to how the character talks or writes.

2) Imagine that you are a sportsperson or a pop star. Write your diary for a week.

What did you do?

What was the weather like?

Who else was with you?

Did anything exciting happen?

How did you feel?

19 Paragraphs

From *Boo!*

She didn't like it at all when her father had to go down to London and, for the first time, she had to sleep alone in the old house.

She went up to her bedroom early. She turned the key and locked the door. She latched the windows and drew the curtains. She peered inside her wardrobe, and pulled open the bottom drawer of her chest-of-drawers; she got down on her knees and looked under the bed.

She undressed; she put on her nightdress.

She pulled back the heavy linen cover and climbed into bed. Not to read but to try and sleep – she wanted to sleep as soon as she could. She reached out and turned off the lamp.

'That's good,' said a little voice. 'Now we're safely locked in for the night.'

Kevin Crossley-Holland

Chat challenge

What is the story about?
Is it a complete story? Can you identify the story structure, e.g. **a beginning, middle, climax, resolution**?
Would it be possible to write it in an even shorter version?
How many paragraphs are there?
What is the subject of each one? Is each paragraph different?
Why do we divide written work into paragraphs?

Comprehension

1) Why was she alone in the house?

2) Why is it important to know that her father was a long way away?

3) Why did she look in her wardrobe and under her bed?

4) What does this tell us about how she felt about being alone?

5) Why is the last line a shock?

6) Does it matter that 'the little voice' is not identified?

 Objective focus

1) This writer has deliberately written a very short story to create a mystery. Make a chart showing what happens in each paragraph.

Paragraph	Subject – what happens
1	
2	
3	
4	
5	

How does this help you to see why the writer has used the paragraphs he has?

2) Change the beginnings of each paragraph by altering the sentence structure, e.g. 'When her father had to …' What difference does this make? Does it make the passage any less scary?

 Links to writing

1) Copy Kevin Crossley-Holland's model and write your own very short story in five paragraphs.

2) Write three more paragraphs.

   A new character arrives.

   Two characters speak.

   A new event occurs.

Assess your understanding

 OK

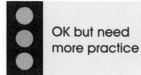 OK but need more practice

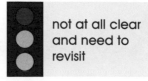 not at all clear and need to revisit

20 What have we learned?

We've learned about **creating and shaping texts** and about **text structure and organisation**.

1 How to use narrative techniques in the first person

- A first-person narrator (**I**) allows us into the head of a character so we see the story through one viewpoint.

- Once you're writing in the first person you should continue in this way or the story won't hang together.

Check understanding!

Find a paragraph written in the third person and rewrite it in the first person. What changes do you find that you have to make?

> First person: **I, me**
> Third person: **he, she, it, they**

2 How to use narrative techniques in the third person

- A third-person narrator (**he, she, it, they**) allows us to observe and comment on a scene and a character and explain a character's thoughts and feelings.

- Once you're writing in the third person you should continue in this way.

Check understanding!

Find a paragraph written in the first person and rewrite it in the third person. What changes do you find that you have to make?

3 How to write formally – instructions

- The writing has to look right (layout) and has to use the right sort of words (special words for the subject). Remember:

- audience not known
- formal vocabulary and no opinions
- use passive tense.

Check understanding!

Look at a letter sent home from school. Highlight all the features of formality within it.

Assess your understanding

 OK

 OK but need more practice

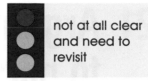 not at all clear and need to revisit

4 How to write formally – biography

Remember:

● use third person ● write in past tense usually in time order ● use pictures or photographs.

Check understanding!

 Choose a famous person. Make a plan for writing a biography. Check you have included all the right features.

5 How to organise texts – diaries

● A diary is written in the first person and includes lots of personal details.

● It is structured by days and uses informal language as it assumes no audience.

● It can switch between past and present tenses.

Check understanding!

Write a diary entry for yesterday and then highlight the features of this type of writing that you have included.

6 How to use paragraphs for pace and emphasis

● In the extreme and for effect, a paragraph **can** be just one sentence.

● It is possible to begin each paragraph in the same way and to change the order of paragraphs for effect.

Check understanding!

 Using the word **paragraph**, write an acrostic mnemonic to help you remember key facts about paragraphs.

21 Argument – using sentences to persuade

Writer is introducing their view

This might be true – it is written to seem like a fact to add weight to the argument

Gives a reason – cause and effect. The use of detail adds weight to the argument

Rhetorical question – does not need an answer – makes it sound obvious

Writer concludes their argument. (Is it the right one?)

Strong title that gives the point of view

This is a fact that can be proved. Gives the impression that the argument is correct

Writer is giving his own view in such a way as to encourage acceptance

Concludes that stage of the point of view

Writer introduces a possible argument against his view

But counters it

Opinion given as fact

BAN SMOKING! IT KILLS!

It is an indisputable fact that smoking causes 120,000 deaths in the UK each year. If we stopped it now, we would save 330 lives per day.

Many well-informed people know that smoking causes more than 40 types of illnesses and has around 20 ways of killing you because cigarettes contain over 400 chemicals, including tar, carbon monoxide (includes cyanide and arsenic) and nicotine. *Therefore*, 30% of all cancer deaths are related to smoking.

Surely you cannot deny the fact that smoking cigarettes increases the chance of suffering a heart attack by two to three times compared to a non-smoker?

Objectors might say that people have a right to decide their own health and we should leave them to smoke if they want to. *But this would be to ignore* the very real dangers of passive smoking which cause several hundred cases of lung cancer and several cases of heart disease in non-smokers in the UK each year. I believe that low tar cigarettes pose an equal threat – so I say it again: … passive smoking is dangerous. Countries which have banned smoking see a huge health gain.

In conclusion, around half of all cigarette smokers will eventually be killed by the habit – as well as other innocent people around them if we do not ban smoking immediately.

Chat challenge

What is the purpose of this piece of writing? What does it aim to do?

How much information does it contain? Which facts grab your attention?

Does the writer use fact or opinion or a mixture of both? For what purpose does the writer use this approach?

Which words make the argument particularly persuasive?

Do the paragraphs in this particular order help?

Comprehension

1) How many people die each year from smoking in the UK?

2) What is in cigarettes that can cause you to become ill?

3) What kinds of diseases can they cause?

4) What is **passive smoking**?

5) What does the writer want doing about the problem?

6) Does the writer's argument convince you? If so, why?

Objective focus

1) Take away the words in italics. Is the passage still an argument? Is it persuasive in any way?

2) Find examples of the following in the passage: using statements of fact, using contrast, using cause and effect, using conditional language (e.g. **If … then**), using repetition, using rhetorical questions, using personal language in the second person (**you**).

3) Using the same features of style, write a passage that argues that children should not be forced to wear school uniform.

Decide what will be in each paragraph.

Think of arguments both for and against.

Find evidence to back up your arguments.

Start each paragraph in a different persuasive way.

Use connectives that help develop your argument, e.g. therefore, however, moreover.

Links to writing

1) Explain how each of the features of style in question 2) of 'Objective focus' helps to create a persuasive argument.

2) Plan a persuasive text to encourage others in your school to support an environmental organisation or event that you think is worthwhile. You may need to do some research on the Internet.

List the main points you want to make.

Collect information to support each point.

Make notes about your audience.

Present your persuasive text in the form of a leaflet.

Publish it with the help of a computer.

Include all the features you have discussed in this passage.

22 Constructing sentences in varied ways 1

From *Cider with Rosie*

It was a world of glass, sparkling and motionless. Vapours had frozen all over the trees and transformed them into confections of sugar. Everything was rigid, locked-up and sealed, and when we breathed the air it smelled like needles and stabbed our nostrils and made us sneeze.

Having sucked a few icicles, and kicked the water-butt – to hear its solid sound – and breathed through the frost on the window-pane, we ran up into the road. We hung around, waiting for something to happen. A dog trotted past like a ghost in a cloud, panting his aura around him. The distant fields in the low weak sun were crumpled like oyster shells.

Presently some more boys came to join us, wrapped like Russians, with multi-coloured noses. We stood round in a group and just gasped at each other, waiting to get an idea. The thin ones were blue, with hunched up shoulders, hands deep in their pockets, shivering. The fat ones were rosy and blowing like whales; all of us had wet eyes. What should we do? We didn't know.

Laurie Lee

Chat challenge

What is the passage describing?
Why doesn't the writer just state the facts?
How many different ways does the writer begin sentences?
Find examples of short sentences. Why does the writer use them?
Find examples of longer sentences. Why does the writer choose to make them longer?
How many comparisons, e.g. **similes**, can you find?

Comprehension

1) What season is the author describing?

2) What does **confections** mean? What kind of thing did the frost on the trees remind the author of?

3) What senses is the author using in his description? Give some examples.

4) What did the dog remind the author of? Why?

5) Why does the author describe the boys as 'wrapped like Russians'?

6) Why do the boys have 'multi-coloured noses'?

7) What does the author really mean by 'It was a world of glass'?

Objective focus

1) Find examples in the passage of where the writer uses other similes or metaphors to develop sentences and make them more interesting.

2) Adverbial phrases normally, but not always, occur at the beginning of a paragraph. Identify the adverbial phrases in the following:

   a. A few minutes earlier, the car had been sparking clean.

   b. When at least we reached the safety of the cave, we dropped down in the sand.

   c. Peering through the window, the prisoner saw the hangman coming to collect him.

3) Use the following as sentence openers.

   a. Slipping in the snow,   **b.** Chomping on an apple,

   c. After a while,   **d.** Without any warning,

Links to writing

1) Write a highly descriptive passage about what you and your friends did in a summer scene, e.g. **at the beach, playing by the side of a river**.

   Paragraph 1: Use a bold opening statement using metaphor. Include descriptive sentences about the scene and what it reminded you of, using more than one sense.

   Paragraph 2: Describe some actions, what you did, what you saw and heard, what things reminded you of …

   Paragraph 3: Some other people join you. What happens? What do they look like or remind you of?

23 Constructing sentences in varied ways 2

Is this how you expect how a book about pets would be written?

The Truth About Pets: Being Owned By a Cat

Playing with cats is a problem. Forget all that stuff about bits of string and catnip. Cats only play with special cat toys. You are their special toy. And this lasts for approximately two minutes – only when you are paying attention. This is to keep you (the 'can-opener') happy; you would be sad if their stomachs were rumbling.

And the thing to remember is that cats are the most intelligent of beasts. One day they will go back to their own planet; consider what they will tell the others about how stupid human beings are.

So … what games do cats play with you? It's never the other way around. Only you think it is.

1. **Cat square-dance**. Cats will sit in defined areas. On mats. On your clean washing. On the steps in front of you. On the most comfortable chair in the garden; this will be the one you want to sit in.

2. **Wet cement**. They will seek it out and mark this territory with their paws.

3. **Keeping an eye on the food cupboard or fridge**. Some days they will just sit there looking cuddly, staring at the food place; big round eyes will make you feel guilty. You know that you have been starving them so you will immediately fill their food bowl.

4. **Bringing you gifts**. These are, in fact, just the remains of their lunch – bits of old mouse or frog; maybe a feather or two if you are lucky. They will be messy – but you will be thrilled by the attention.

Such is the way cats own us.

Chat challenge

Who is the audience for this kind of book?
Why do you think the writer chose to write differently?
Do you find anything in the tone of the writing amusing or unusual? Why?
Find examples of short sentences. Why does the writer use them?
Find examples of longer sentences. Why does the writer choose to make them longer?
Find examples of when the writer does not use complete sentences. Why does the writer do this?

Comprehension

1) Name two things people normally use to play with cats.

2) Why does the author say that these do not work?

3) Explain why cats would call their owners 'can-openers'?

4) What is the effect of the cats staring at the food cupboard or fridge?

5) What kinds of 'gifts' might cats bring their owners? What state would they be in?

6) Explain the joke in the title: 'Being Owned By a Cat'.

Objective focus

1) In this passage the author constructs shorter, more factual sentences to give information and to create a jokey effect for your age group. Rewrite the information as you would in a traditional non-fiction book. Which is the more interesting version for your age group? Why?

2) Use connectives to join the sentences in the first paragraph into one or two longer ones. Does the effect of the writing change?

3) Why does the writer start some of the sentences with 'And'?

4) Look at the short sentences in the numbered points. Rewrite these as one or two long sentences. What happens to the effect of the writer even if the facts do not change?

5) Find examples of where the author uses semi-colons. They act like a balance, with one idea on each side. Write three sentences about cats using the same technique.

Links to writing

1) Write your own 'The Truth About Pets' page for some animal behaviours that need explaining to younger children.

   Choose an animal that they will know. Think about the kind of things they do.

   Decide what will go in each paragraph.

   Find out the real animal facts.

   Use informal rather than formal language.

   Keep the sentences short.

   Use semicolons to create sentences that are jokes.

2) Publish your page, using the computer and any visuals that you can find.

3) See how successful you have been. Test the story on younger children: did they like it? Did they find it easy to understand?

24 Colons or semicolons

From *Walkabout*

*In this novel, two children are stranded in the Australian desert after their plane crashes. They meet a Native Australian – an **aboriginal** – who is 'on walkabout'.*

The desert was neither flat nor monotonous; nor was it like so many other deserts – the Gobi, the Steppes, or certain parts of the Sahara – featureless and devoid of colour. Its formation was varied: patches of sand, outcrops of rock, dried up watercourses, salt-pans, faults, and frequent belts of vegetation. And its colours were strong: bold and harsh and sharply defined: belts of yellow, blocks of bottle-green, patches of fire flame-red, and fields of blood …

Later, when collecting food, the children meet the boy …

The girl's first impulse was to grab Peter and run; but as her eyes swept over the stranger, her fear died slowly away. The boy was young – certainly no older than she was; he was unarmed, and his attitude was more inquisitive than threatening: more puzzled than hostile.

He wasn't the least bit like an African Negro. His skin was certainly black, but beneath it was a curious hint of under-surface bronze, and it was fine-grained: glossy, satiny, almost silk-like. His hair wasn't crinkly but nearly straight; and his eyes were blue-black: big, soft and enquiring. In his hand was a baby rock wallaby, its eyes, unclosed in death, staring vacantly above a tiny pointed snout.

James Vance Marshall

Chat challenge

From which two punctuation marks is a semicolon made? How is a semicolon different from a comma or a full stop?

From which two punctuation marks is a colon made? How is a colon different from a comma or a full stop?

Why not use a comma or a full stop? What extra do semicolons or colons add to the meaning or effect of a passage?

Identify all the semicolons and the colons in the passage. Would you have used different punctuation? Why?

Can you identify any rules for the use of semicolons and colons?

Comprehension

1) Why was this desert different from other ones?

2) What was noticeable about the desert's colours?

3) When she first saw the Aborigine boy, what was the girl's first reaction? Why did she not do this?

4) What is the name of the boy?

5) What does the girl notice about the Aborigine boy's skin and his hair?

6) What was the Aborigine boy holding?

Objective focus

1) Colons introduce a list of items or can say, 'I am going to tell you more about what I have just said.' Find examples in the passage to prove this definition.

2) Complete these sentences after the colon with suitable information.

   a. The jungle was amazing: …

   b. This was what was underneath her bed: …

3) Sometimes writers use colons to balance two parts of a sentence. Rewrite these two examples using a colon:

   a. The enemy was advancing. Defeat was certain.

   b. He felt really pleased with himself. Everything was going well in his life.

4) Semicolons are used instead of full stops to separate two closely-linked main clauses of similar importance, or to break up long and complicated items in a list. Find an example in the passage to prove this definition.

Links to writing

1) Write a description of a landscape like the one in the first paragraph. You could find pictures and information on the Internet, e.g. **what is Antarctica like?** Use colons to introduce, and expand upon, the detail.

2) Write a description of a character in this landscape – as in the details given about the Aborigine in the third paragraph. Use colons to introduce, and expand upon, the detail.

3) Describe an exciting chase in this landscape. Use a long sentence to build tension, but divide it using semicolons. Ask a friend to check your work and comment on whether you have been successful.

25 Dashes or brackets

From *Pickwick Papers*

In this story, set in Victorian times, Mr Jingle speaks in a very strange way. He is just about to travel on an open-topped coach, drawn by horses.

'Any luggage, Sir?' enquired the coachman.

'Who – I? Brown paper parcel here, that's all – other luggage gone by water – packing cases, nailed up – big as houses – heavy, very heavy,' replied the stranger, as he forced into his pocket as much as he could of the brown paper parcel, which presented suspicions of containing one shirt and a handkerchief.

'Heads, heads, take care of your heads,' cried the stranger, as they came out under the low archway, which in those days formed the entrance to the coach-yard. 'Terrible place – dangerous work – other day – five children – mother – tall lady, eating sandwiches – forgot the arch – crash – knock – children look round – mother's head off – sandwich in her hand – no mouth to put it in – head of a family off – shocking, shocking – eh, sir, eh?'

Charles Dickens

Chat challenge

What do you notice immediately about the look of the final paragraph when dashes are used?
What kind of effect does it give when you read it?
Is it amusing? Why?
Why not use full stops or commas? What would be the effect of this?
What impression does this use of this punctuation give us of the character of Mr Jingle?
Can you tell things about people's characters by the way that they speak?

Comprehension

1) What did Mr Jingle's luggage consist of?

2) What does Mr Jingle say about the rest of his luggage?

3) Do you believe Mr Jingle? Why?

4) What makes Mr Jingle tell people to 'take care of your heads'?

5) What story does Mr Jingle tell about what happened the 'other day'?

6) Is the story tragic or comic?

7) What might it say about Mr Jingle that he tells such stories?

Objective focus

1) Dashes separate ideas. Rewrite the second paragraph using complete sentences to describe the same event. How does this change the effect?

2) Brackets and dashes enable writers to add more information. Add more information in the brackets to these sentences.

    a. The old man (…), left his money to the cats' home.

    b. We faced another day of snow (…).

    c. Fry the onions, add the carrots (…) and cook for two minutes.

3) Read the following sentences. Rewrite them as one sentence using brackets and dashes.

    a. I wanted to become a gospel singer.

    b. I had always sung gospel music with my father.

    c. He used to sing back home in Jamaica.

    d. I joined a choir in south London.

Links to writing

1) Rewrite Mr Jingle's first speech, but this time give extra information in brackets about the detail. Why had his other luggage gone by water? Why were the cases very heavy? What difference does this make to the effect of the writing?

2) Make notes about events from your past. Add information to make the recount more interesting. Use brackets for this.

3) Develop the notes you made for question 2) into a part of your autobiography and publish it using a computer.

26 Punctuation clarifying meaning

Read the examples carefully.

What difference does the punctuation make to the meaning?

Chat challenge

Look carefully at the examples. What are the differences in punctuation between each one?

How does the different punctuation change the meaning in each case?

What is the effect of this?

What would happen to the meaning if you took away all the punctuation?

Comprehension

1) How do these examples show that it is important to use punctuation carefully?

2) How could some of the examples be very confusing if you were just speaking them?

3) How could you emphasise the correct punctuation if you were speaking these statements?

4) Why does it make some of these statements amusing? Give reasons.

Objective focus

1) Use hyphens to join these words together in at least two different ways to create different meanings. Write the words in sentences to show the differences in meaning.

   a. hot water tap   **b.** fifty dollar notes

   c. grand piano salesman

2) Rewrite these sentences using different punctuation to give at least two different meanings. Explain how each is different.

   a. We order merchandise and sell the products.

   b. Have your car serviced today free. Oil included.

   c. I shall buy a car, in part-exchange for my wife.

   d. The teachers said Emma should be quiet.

   e. We give quality service and attention to detail.

Links to writing

1) Punctuate these in two ways to mean two very different things.

   a. DANGER

   NO

   SKATING ALLOWED

   b. Come and eat Fred said mum.

   c. Can you see Fred called Max through the fog?

   d. Don't use commas which are not necessary.

2) Write a story in which confusion over punctuation leads to a very embarrassing situation. You could use one of the examples above.

27 Speech

From *The Machine Gunners*

This story takes place in the Second World War. Chas listens to his parents talk about a bombing.

'I thought we were a gonner last night, I really did. That dive bomber … I thought it was going to land on top of the shelter … Mrs Spalding had one of her turns.'

'It wasn't a dive bomber,' announced Father with authority. 'It had two engines. He came down on the rooftops 'cos one of the RAF lads was after him. Right on his tail. You could see his guns firing. And he got him. Crashed on the old laundry at Chirton. Full bomb load. I felt the heat on me face a mile away.' Mother's face froze.

'Nobody killed, love. That laundry's been empty for years. Just as well – there's not much left of it.'

Chas finished his last carefully-cut slice of fried bread and looked hopefully at his father.

'Can I go and see it?'

'Aye, you can go and look. But you won't find nowt but bricks. Everything just went.'

Mother looked doubtful. 'D'you think he should?'

'Let him go, lass. There's nowt left.'

'No unexploded bombs?'

'No, a quiet night really. Lots of our fighters up. That's why you didn't hear any guns.'

Robert Westall

Chat challenge

What special punctuation do you need to punctuate speech?
Why do you think this is necessary?
How should speech be set out when you are writing it?
How do you know who is speaking in the passage, even if their names are not written down?
Which words tell you how the characters might have spoken the words?
Do any words tell you how the characters may have felt?

Comprehension

1) Who are the people speaking in this passage? What tells you this?

2) What evidence is there to show that this story is set in the Second World War?

3) Why do you think Chas is so keen to have a look at the crashed plane?

4) Why do his parents let him go in the end?

5) What slang words can you find in the passage?

6) Why is it permitted to use non-standard English in speech but not in other kinds of writing?

Objective focus

1) Rewrite the last section of the dialogue, but write who said the words, e.g. **said Mother, replied Father**. How does this make a difference in the speech? Does it slow it down? Does it make it seem too obvious?

2) Write a piece of dialogue between two friends which only uses their words in speech marks and does not comment on them or how they said the words, e.g. no **said Fred, replied Tracy**. What information do you have to include in the speech to make sure the reader gets the correct impression?

3) Rewrite the speech from question 2) using standard English. How does this make a difference? How much of a sense of the characters or the place do you lose?

4) Chas 'looked hopefully'. His mother 'looked doubtful'. How do these clues help us to read the tone of the speech and understand how the characters were feeling? Choose some different words to include. Does the speech have to be changed to make their new feelings clear?

Links to writing

1) Continue the dialogue in the scene, following the same style and the same use of language.

   Make sure that Chas' mum expresses some more concerns about him going.

   Chas has to defend himself and his father supports him.

   What warnings would his parents give him?

2) Write a new scene of dialogue using some of the things you have discussed from the extract. In the book, Chas finds the German who was piloting the crashed plane.

Assess your understanding OK   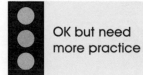 OK but need more practice   not at all clear and need to revisit

28 What have we learned?

We've revisited **sentence structure and punctuation.**

1 How to use sentences to persuade in argument

Persuasive techniques include:

- statements of fact/ technical language
- emotive language
- use of opinion as fact
- connectives
- questions – often rhetorical
- using language in the second person.

Check understanding!

 Make a list of all the things you **wouldn't** do in a piece of writing to persuade someone. What would really set them against you and your views?

2 How to construct sentences in varied ways 1

For a descriptive, poetic effect use:

- similes and metaphors
- alliteration
- powerful adjectives, adverbs
- adverbial phrases to create a sense of time.

Check understanding!

 Write three poetic similes and three metaphors – then use them in your writing.

3 How to construct sentences in varied ways 2

For information presented in a jokey way:

- use short, factual sentences
- use **And** and **Or** at the beginning of sentences
- use ellipses …
- use informal language.

Check understanding!

 Write a list of all the things you know about how to make writing funny for your audience. For each item on your list give an example.

And another thing …

Assess your understanding

 OK

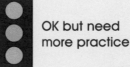 OK but need more practice

 not at all clear and need to revisit

4 How to use colons and semicolons

- Use a colon to introduce a list.
- Use semicolons to separate clauses, or items in a list.

Check understanding!

 Write out a list of all the things you need or are going to do next week. Check for the correct use of colons and semicolons.

5 How to use dashes – and (brackets)

- A dash can be used in informal writing to add an extra bit of information.
- Brackets can also be used to add extra information.

Check understanding!

 Find a piece of your writing from science or history. Rewrite it using dashes and brackets to either add more serious and accurate information or to make it funny.

6 How to use punctuation to clarify meaning

- Punctuation is the way in which you tell a reader how to read your text.

Check understanding!

 Write three powerful hyphenated words that you would use in descriptive, poetic writing. Then three that you would use for comic effect. Then use them!

the tear-stained face of the girl

7 How to use speech marks

- Speech marks show when a character is speaking.
- Speech is often broken up with information about who is speaking so then you need two sets of speech marks.

Check understanding!

 Write out five challenging sentences with speech but no punctuation and give them to a friend. Make sure you have got the correct versions written out for checking.

Glossary

apostrophe   a punctuation mark (') used to indicate either possession or the omission of letters or numbers

autobiography   the story of someone's life, written by themselves

balanced argument   looking at an issue or topic from different points of view and then reaching a conclusion. Sometimes called a discussion

biography   the story of a person's life

colon   a punctuation mark (:) used to introduce a list or a sentence or phrase taken from somewhere else

derivation   where something has come from

diary   a book giving the days of the year in which someone writes down their appointments or what happens each day

first person   I, me, my, myself, mine (singular) and we, us, our, ourselves and ours (plural)

hypothesis   a suggestion or theory that tries to explain something but has not been proved right

imagery   the use of words to produce pictures in the mind of the reader

journalistic writing   news stories or articles for a newspaper or magazine, radio, TV or Internet

mnemonic   anything that helps us to remember something else

narrative   the recounting or telling of past events; account, chronicle, description, list, story, news report, statement

paragraph   groups of sentences that are all about the same topic separated from the rest of the text by a space above and below it or by indenting the first line (leaving a space between the margin and the first word). A paragraph usually contains sentences that deal with one topic, and a new paragraph signals a change of topic.

perspective   someone's viewpoint or opinion

punctuation   the symbols used in written language to indicate the end of a sentence or a clause, or to indicate that it is a question, etc

. , ; : ? ! ' - ' ' ( )   are the punctuation symbols most commonly used in English

reported speech   what someone else said, but without using the exact words, e.g. He said that he was going to come. (The person's exact words were 'I'm going to come.')

rhetorical   A rhetorical question is really a statement that is not expecting an answer. Rhetorical questions can be used for persuasive effect.

semicolon   a punctuation mark (;) used in formal writing between two parts of a sentence, usually when each part could form sentences themselves. They can also be used to separate items in a list.

speculation   guessing about something to form an opinion

speech marks   punctuation marks (' ') that show us when a character is speaking

supposition   something someone supposes but does not know for sure

third person   he, she or it, his, hers, its, him, her, himself, herself, itself (singular); they, them, theirs, themselves (plural)

viewpoint   somebody's perspective or opinion

Year 6 Literacy topics

Narrative	Fiction genres	Extending narrative	Authors and texts	Short stories with flashbacks
Non-fiction	Biography and autobiography	Journalistic writing	Argument	Formal/impersonal writing
Poetry	The power of imagery		Finding a voice	
Revision	Reading and writing narrative (and plays)	Reading and writing non-fiction	Reading poetry	

Handy hints

Six tips on handwriting

1) Space out letters, words and sentences evenly.

2) Keep the size of your letters even.

3) Write on the lines if you are writing on lined paper or keep straight if you are not.

4) Make sure that your pen or pencil is comfortable (and that the pencil is sharp).

5) Use an eraser (rubber, correction fluid or correction pen) if you make a mistake.

6) If **you** can't read it then the chances are that neither can anyone else. Keep it neat all the time.

Rules for capital letters

Use capital letters for:

- people's names
- people's titles (like Mrs Jones)
- places
- days of the week
- months of the year
- organisations.

Full stops

Always put a full stop at the end of a sentence unless you are using a ? or a !

My part of East London has a character all its own. There is a collection of streets, parallel to each other, leading back from the old railway line .

The crumbling terraced houses are full of life, even if they look old. Above them are the Docklands Light Railway lines.

Huge concrete pillars hold up these tracks. They remind me of enormous grey legs striding across the city.

The driverless trains on them are like blue caterpillars crawling slowly on their way to find somewhere to rest underneath the railway arches.

These arches make a new little world. In between the pillars, the spaces have been cleverly used. Some spaces have been bricked in and walls divide them into workshops or dark offices.

Spelling

Five tips on spelling

1) Make sure you know these words because these are the words that are most often misspelled in tests:

advertise	attempts	change	designed	future
individual	injured	known	nastiest	perfectly
produce	ready	regardless	serious	surprise
stripes	swimming	technique	themselves	vanishing

2) Keep using *look, say, cover, write, check.*

3) Try writing tricky words in sentences to help you remember them in a context.

4) Try splitting a word into syllables to work out each section.

5) Give it a go even if you are not sure.

OH! And don't always rely on the spellchecker when working on screen – keep thinking for yourself so that when you are writing you don't get stuck.

OH! And don't spell the word right but then get the apostrophe wrong because that makes the whole thing wrong. Use the apostrophe to show you who owns what (**Ben's dinner**), for groups of people (**The Rising Stars' offices**) and to make two words into one (**I am** = **I'm**).

Rising Stars UK Ltd, 22 Grafton Street, London W1S 4EX

www.risingstars-uk.com

Acknowledgements

Unit 8 page 18 – Extract from 'American Folk Rhyme' adapted by William Cole from *Word Games*, Sandy Brownjohn and Janet Whitaker, Hodder and Stoughton

Unit 9 page 20 – Adapted extract from *Shooting the Elephant* by George Orwell, 1950. Reprinted by permission of AM Heath & Co Ltd. For the estate of the late George Orwell and for the publisher Martin Secker & Warburg Ltd.

Unit 10 page 22 http://www.cool-reads.co.uk Review is by Jordan Sandford from Barnet, London.
Soccer Mad cover image reprinted by permission of Random House Ltd.

Unit 11 page 24 – William Shakespeare, ROMEO AND JULIET, edited by Philip Page and Marilyn Pettit. Shakespeare Graphics (Hodder Murray, 1999), illustrations © 1999 by Philip Page. Reproduced in adapted form by permission of the illustrator and Hodder Education

Unit 12 page 26 – Extract from *Little House in the Big Woods* by Laura Ingalls Wilder, Methuen Children's Books

Unit 14 page 30 – Extract from *Animorphs 1, The Invasion* by K A Applegate, 1997. Scholastic Ltd

Unit 15 page 32 – Extract from *Warrior Scarlet* by Rosemary Sutcliff, published by Oxford University Press and Puffin. Reprinted with permission of David Higham Associates

Unit 17 page 36 – Extract from *Hannah Goslar Remembers* by Alison Leslie Gold, published by Bloomsbury

Unit 18 page 38 – Extract from *Zlata's Diary: A Child's Life in Sarajevo* by Zlata Filipovic, translated by Christina Pribichevich-Zoric (Viking 1994, first published in France as 'Le Journal de Zlata' by Fixot et editions Robert Laffont 1993). Copyright © Fixot et editions Robert Laffont 1993. Reproduced by permission of Penguin Books Ltd.

Unit 19 page 40 – 'Boo!' by Kevin Crossley-Holland from *Short! A Book of Very Short Stories* (OUP, 1998), copyright © Kevin Crossley-Holland 1998, reprinted by permission of Oxford University Press

Unit 22 page 46 – Extract from *Cider with Rosie* by Laurie Lee, published by The Hogarth Press. Reprinted by permission of The Random House Group Ltd.

Unit 24 page 50 – Extract from *Walkabout* by James Vance Marshall (first published as *The Children* by Michael Joseph, 1959). Copyright © James Vance Marshall, 1969. Reproduced by permission of Penguin Books Ltd

Unit 27 page 56 – Extract from *The Machine Gunners* by Robert Westall, published by Macmillan Children's Books, London, UK

All facts are correct at time of going to press.

Published 2007

Text, design and layout © Rising Stars UK Ltd.

Design and illustration: HL Studios

Editorial project management: Dodi Beardshaw

Editorial: Dodi Beardshaw

Cover design: Burville-Riley Design

British Library Cataloguing in Publication Data.

A CIP record for this book is available from the British Library.

ISBN: 978-1-84680-099-3

Printed by: Gutenberg Press, Malta